Kid Sitter Basics
A Handbook for Babysitters

Celeste Stuhring, R.N.
Glen T. Stuhring, M.D.*

*Certified by the American Academy of Fami~~~~~~~~~~s.

D1472707

Printed in the United States of America.

Library of Congress Cataloging-in-Publication Data

Stuhring, Celeste
    Kid Sitter Basics: a handbook/Celeste Stuhring. p. cm.
    Includes bibliographical references.
    ISBN: 0-9676448-0-1
    1. Babysitting–Handbooks, manuals, etc.–Juvenile literature.

I. Title.
HQ769.5.S78 1994
649'. 1'0248-dc20   93-40673
                          CIP
                          AC

The Kid Sitter Basics handbook contains general guidelines for babysitters. This handbook is not meant to replace certified courses in babysitting, first aid and CPR, which all babysitters are urged to take, but should be used as a tool to accompany these courses. Although the manual contains information from America's most-respected safety, first aid, and CPR organizations, no booklet can substitute for the advice of a physician or trained healthcare provider. Be sure to contact a health professional should an accident or injury occur.

Kid Safety Plus assumes no liability for any actions taken by persons based on information given in this book.

For more information on *Kid Sitter Basics*, to order additional booklets and materials or for information on group rate discounts, e-mail Celeste at Jimassea@aol.com

Dear Babysitter,

Welcome to *Kid Sitter Basics*! This handbook is designed to help you become a better and safer babysitter. We've enhanced this latest version to incorporate our many years of medical experience with the most up-to-date practical information. In addition to providing you essential safety information and valuable babysitting tips, it will also help you with the business end of what may be your first job.

As a babysitter, you play a very important role in the lives of the families you serve. Children often become very attached to their babysitters and remember their stories, games and tender loving care for years to come. You may prevent children from being injured or disabled, and might even save a child's life by applying the common sense knowledge and first aid contained in this handbook.

You deserve thanks for taking your job seriously and learning as much as you can about babysitting. Enjoy *Kid Sitter Basics*—and your new job taking care of children!

Celeste Stuhring, R.N.

Glen T. Stuhring M.D.

Celeste Stuhring is a Registered Nurse and Neonatal Nurse Specialist who has spent over 15 years caring for infants and children. She collaborated with her husband, Dr. Glen T. Stuhring, a family doctor, to produce a book that babysitters could take with them on the job. The mother of two active boys, Celeste is also the owner of Kid Safety Plus, which offers community education, first-aid courses and self-help booklets for parents, teenagers and day care providers.

This manual is dedicated to my sons, Tyler and Matthew. Their contributions have been invaluable to the writing of this book. I'd also like to recognize all the great babysitters who have taken care of Tyler and Matthew over the years—their patience, love for children and willingness to help has made this book possible.

Consultants:
American Academy of Family Practice Physicians

Project Management and Editing:
Candy Young and the Staff @ Young & Company
Bellevue, Washington

Art:
Barbara Stuhring
Meg Clement

Design:
Karen Peters
Red Barn Design
Kirkland, Washington

Table of Contents

What's a good age to start babysitting?

Many health and safety agencies
recommend that pre-teens start
babysitting around 11-12 years of age.
However, age is not the only factor to
consider. Regardless of age, a babysitter
must be mature. If you are motivated to
try new experiences, learn about taking
care of children safely, not afraid to ask
questions, can work well with adults and
children, and are confident about taking
on responsibility, then you're ready to
learn more about babysitting. You should
begin with a babysitting class to get more
information about what it takes to babysit.
Remember this is a job. In order to be
successful, you need the support of your
parents to help you get the resources and
experiences you need to be a great sitter.

Getting Started

Why babysit?

Babysitting is a lot of fun. It's an exciting opportunity to start your first job. You get to be around small children, and you can also earn extra spending money or begin saving for college.

While babysitting can be fun, it's also a big responsibility. Think about it. **To parents, their child is the most important being in their entire lives! That's why it's important to learn everything you can about basic childcare and safety.**

In addition to teaching you about personal safety and first aid, this booklet will help

prepare you for your first job. You'll learn what to expect in children of different ages and how to keep them happy. You'll also gain ideas for preparing easy meals and learn some fun, new games to play.

Should I babysit?

Do you like being with children? If you don't, maybe it's better to think about mowing lawns, walking pets or washing cars. But if you genuinely like to spend time with children, and you feel comfortable with responsibility, then you're probably ready to start babysitting.

Parents want a sitter who is honest and trustworthy, as well as someone who will follow their instructions carefully and obey rules. They want a sitter who will keep their child safe and happy, is flexible, and can adapt to the changing needs of children.

Children have their own ideas about what they want in a sitter. They want someone who is kind and cheerful, someone who will play with them and be a good listener.

Basically, children want someone who is like an adult, in that they are dependable and make good decisions, yet is also like a kid so they can have fun, too.

A good way to find out if you will like babysitting is to accompany an older friend or family member during a sit or volunteer at a church, nursery or preschool. You'll learn all sorts of important things on the job, and you'll feel more confident about how to behave. You'll also be able to say you have experience when looking for your own babysitting jobs. If you like children and are responsible, then you're probably ready to start babysitting.

Before your first job . . .

Sit down with your parents before you begin looking for a job. Your babysitting could have a big impact on your family, so you'll need to make sure your work fits in with the needs of everyone else. Your parents can help you decide if you have the skills for babysitting and also if you have the time. Before you look for a job, ask your parents to help you answer these questions:

❏ 1   What days of the week can I babysit?

❏ 2   What hours can I sit during the day?

❏ 3   How late can I babysit at night?

❏ 4   What ages of children should I sit for?

❏ 5   How many children should I watch by myself?

❏ 6   How much should I charge per hour?

❏ 7   Should I charge an additional fee for babysitting more than one child?

❏ 8   Should I charge a special rate for family friends?

❏ 9   Who should I approach for my first job?

❏ 10   How can I get some experience with children?

❏ 11   Can you help me think of things to do with the children I watch?

❏ 12   Do you think I'm ready to cook a meal for another family?

❏ 13   Where can I get experience taking care of infants?

❏ 14   How should I advertise my sitting services?

❏ 15   How do I get to and from jobs?

❏ 16   Do you think I'm ready to perform first aid if necessary?

❏ 17   What should I do if I don't feel safe? How can I let you know?

❏ 18   What should I do if a child refuses to obey or has a tantrum?

❏ 19   What if I have homework? When should I do it?

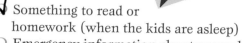

Don't leave home without your...

It is important to be well prepared for a babysitting job. Wear simple, comfortable clothing, including a jacket if needed, and bring a backpack or tote bag containing these basic items:

- Note paper
- Pencil or pen
- Sitter calendar (so you're ready to schedule future jobs)
- Snack and beverage
- Kid Sitter Basics Handbook

- Something to read or homework (when the kids are asleep)
- Emergency information about yourself
- Handy flashlight and your house key
- *Optional items:* a small first aid kit and portable radio

Be creative!

Your creativity can help make you a popular sitter with the kids you watch. Put together a "Goody Bag" that includes a few special things for times when kids get bored. Look for free items from local health stores and children's fairs. Think of a special story or song that fits with the season—something about autumn coming, or Valentine's Day, or a new joke. Children are easily entertained by all sorts of funny little things. Your "goodies" don't have to be expensive. You might want to share a kid-appropriate movie, or bring a book or music from home. Just make sure they're safe for the age of the child you're watching.

If you're not sure, ask the parents. Keep notes about which goodies are popular.

Here are some ideas for your goody bag:

- ★ *Craft supplies:* Blunt scissors, tape, water soluble markers, glue, craft paper, etc.
- ★ Coloring books, drawing paper and crayons
- ★ Dolls, stuffed animals, puppets, stickers or cars
- ★ Puzzles, comics or playing cards
- ★ Board games such as Candyland, Checkers, Life or Monopoly
- ★ Favorite books containing poems, silly jokes or fairy tales

You're more prepared than you think

You probably already know a lot of things that will come in handy when you babysit. It's a good idea to write them down so you can talk about your skills when it's time to meet babysitting clients. Think about what you liked when you were a kid and what you like now.

Do you enjoy games? ★ Do you play Checkers, peek-a-boo, hide 'n' seek, or

cards? ★ What are your favorite outdoor games? ★ Favorite indoor games? ★ Do you like to read? Young children might also enjoy some of your favorite books. ★ What can you cook without help from your parents? (Examples: macaroni and cheese, soup or grilled cheese sandwiches) ★ What kinds of snacks do you like? ★ What songs or crafts do you know? ★ Can you draw or do origami?

Don't oversell your skills

When babysitting, it's important to tell a parent if you've never done a task before. Sometimes sitters are so eager to babysit that they don't want to admit they don't know how to do something.

Don't be afraid to tell parents if you don't feel qualified for certain jobs such as cooking, using appliances, watching kids in or around water, bathing children, watching or walking pets, changing a diaper, or other tasks. Most of these skills take practice and lessons before you can add these talents to your resume. If a parent asks you to do something you don't know how to do or are uncomfortable doing, tell them you can't be responsible for that activity.

TIPS FOR FUN!

Hang out together, talk & get to know each other

Going Into Business

You're ready to find your very first babysitting job. But, how do you get the phone to ring? It's not as hard as you think. Almost any family with small children needs a babysitter every now and then. You just need to let them know you're available!

Spread the word that you're ready once your parents give you approval. Tell your relatives, friends, and teachers, and ask them to recommend you for babysitting jobs. Introduce yourself to neighbors with children, or people you see with kids at the playground. Don't be shy. If you're polite and business-like, adults will think it's quite normal that you're approaching them about a job.

Get creative. Make a flyer stating your name, age, availability, phone number, and babysitting abilities. Then distribute your flyers to neighbors, post on the church bulletin board, or give to your parents to take to their friends at work. But, before distributing your flyers, be sure to have your parents review the flyer, and get their permission for where and when to hand them out.

Here's an example of a flyer:

Reliable Babysitter!

13-year-old will provide loving, safe care for your children after school or on weekends. Successfully completed a certified babysitting course. Reasonable rates!

Call Mary Anne at 555-1234.

You can also check with your local community's school office. Many schools keep a list of students who have taken a babysitting course or will make referrals for honor students when parents call looking for a babysitter. They are usually happy to put your name on their list if you have approval from your parents.

Comfort in numbers

You may want to get together with a few friends and cover for each other on babysitting jobs. That way, if you're not available to babysit when a parent calls, you can provide your clients with another sitter's number. Be sure to let your friends know that you'll be available as a backup to them, too. Sharing jobs with other sitters is also helpful if you get sick and need a replacement.

References

Sometimes new customers want the names of references, which are people who know you and can reassure the parent that you'll be a reliable babysitter. The best people to use as references are people you have babysat for in the past. Ask past clients if they would mind if you give their name as a reference. Other good people to ask are neighbors and family friends.

Handling the business

Babysitting is a business, just like delivering newspapers or working in a store. It involves payment for services given. You must be prepared to handle the business aspects of babysitting in a professional, confident manner. Here are some suggestions.

"Can you babysit for us?"
The phone rings. Mrs. Jones wants you to babysit. What do you do?

First of all, don't accept jobs from total strangers. Ask the person how they found out about you. Then ask your parents' help in checking them out before you say yes or no.

You'll need to know...
When someone asks you to babysit, write down the following information:

- ☞ Parents' full name with correct spelling
- ☞ Parents' address
- ☞ Parents' phone number
- ☞ Names and ages of children
- ☞ Date and time you'll be working
- ☞ Extra duties, like feeding the children
- ☞ How you will get to and from the job
- ☞ How they heard about you

If this is your first time babysitting for the family, discuss your rates. It's really important to let the family know how much you charge so you can avoid any uncomfortable situations at the end of a job.

Ask if you can come 20-30 minutes early to meet the family, fill out your "First Visit" babysitter forms (see "The First Visit" chapter in this handbook) and get special instructions.

Keep a sitter calendar

Keep a special calendar for your babysitting jobs, or write down your appointments on the family calendar. Consult both your babysitting calendar and parents before you agree to babysit.

When you take a babysitting job, always write in the appropriate day on your calendar. Also be sure to write the name of the family, time of sit, and phone number.

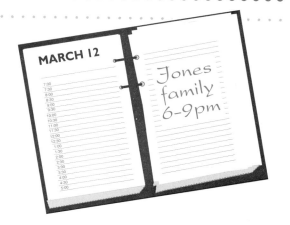

Who decides my rates?

Some of your customers will be accustomed to hiring babysitters and will offer you the rate they pay everyone else. Others will not be familiar with babysitting fees in the area. Some customers will expect you to know what to charge.

What do I charge?

Babysitting rates differ. In some cities they are much higher than others. Different neighborhoods often have different rates. Ask around in your neighborhood. Ask your parents and family friends what they pay sitters. Be sure to find out what people your age and with your experience charge. Older babysitters will often charge more than inexperienced sitters. Many full-time sitters charge more than occasional evening sitters. Some sitters charge more after midnight if they stay up. Some charge less if they are allowed to go to sleep. You may decide to charge an additional fee for taking care of more than two children, doing  extra chores or staying longer hours.

The most important thing to remember is to establish your rates before taking the job. This helps avoid awkward situations when the job is over. Consider every job unique, and be fair and charge according to your responsibilities.

Discuss the question of rates with your parents. Decide on a rate that's fair for everyone. If you charge more than everyone else does, you won't get many jobs. If you charge less, you're probably not being fair to yourself, and will send the message that you lack self-confidence.

When a new customer calls, be sure to discuss your rates on the telephone. If they don't ask what you charge, don't be shy—tell them! You can do this very politely by saying in a matter-of-fact tone of voice, "By the way, I charge two dollars an hour." If your rates are fair, your customer will not be offended. They'll actually be relieved that you're acting like a professional businessperson.

First-time sitters are often shy about asking adults for payment. If you think it will help, practice with your parents so you'll have confidence in getting paid at the end of the job. The more sitting jobs you do, the easier it will be to collect payment.

In a hurry…

If the parents are in a rush and aren't able to help you fill out the "First Visit" form just try to do your best. Ask them questions, especially important information like where you can find emergency phone numbers. Get instructions on meals and bedtime. Be sure to write down where the parents can be reached in case you need to check with them while on the job. **Ask questions and write things down!** The more you know about the family, the better the job will go, which decreases the chance for mistakes. After the job, ask the parents when they'll have time to go over the "First Visit" form so you're better prepared for the next time you babysit.

The First Job

Congratulations! You've just landed for your first babysitting job! Now you need to find out as much as possible about the family so you can adjust to their routine and learn the household rules.

If the parents agree, come early on your first job so you can get specific information to help you each time you babysit. We've prepared a suggested "First Visit" form, located in the back of this manual, to use as a guideline. It will take you about 20-30 minutes to fill out. Make photocopies of the "First Visit" form to use for all of your babysitting clients. Keep the form in a safe place when you get home—so you'll be prepared for your next job!

What to do on your first visit with a new family:

➼ Meet the children, parents, and pets, and find out the children's names and ages.

➼ Have the parents fill out the appropriate information on the "First Visit" form.

➼ Locate bathrooms, bedrooms, telephones and all playing areas.

➼ If you need to change the children's clothes, such as at bedtime, locate the clothing for each child. For infants, locate the diapers and changing areas. If you've never changed a diaper before, or if you don't know how to use either cloth or disposable diapers, have the parent show you how.

➼ Locate all exits, and determine how to lock doors and windows. Locate smoke alarms, flashlights and other items.

➼ Check for first aid supplies, and make sure emergency phone numbers are by the phone.

➼ Are you preparing a meal? Get specific instructions. How do you work the appliances? Note eating areas and learn what snacks and drinks are available. What foods are off-limits for the children? What food is available for you?

➼ Learn home guidelines for discipline, phone messages, playtime, TV, games, visitors, bed times, off-limit areas and outdoor play.

➼ What can you do with the children that they would enjoy? What activities do the kids like to do?

➼ Determine any special conditions the children have that you should know about, such as allergies, illness, medications or behavior problems.

If you don't understand how to do something, ask the parent to show you how and write down the answer.

While on the job give your full attention to the kids.

TIPS FOR FUN!
---> Play "20 Questions" to get to know each other better

On the Job

Before the parents leave

Every home and every job is going to provide new challenges and experiences. Even if you and the parents have filled out the "First Visit" form, there are many things that will change with each babysitting job. For each job, be sure to talk with the parents before they leave.

Note situations such as a sick child, new rules, visiting relatives or friends. If you are asked to give any medication, get specific instructions in writing.

If the parents are planning a very late evening, let them know that you may have trouble staying awake. If you're working at a late evening job or spending the night, find out from the parent where you should sleep.

For each babysitting job, be sure to find out the following:

- ♥ Where will the parents be? (Write down the address and phone number.)
- ♥ What time will they be home?
- ♥ Can you contact the parents if you need help or advice?
- ♥ If you're unable to reach the parents, is there a neighbor you can ask for assistance?
- ♥ Will the parents check in at regular intervals?
- ♥ Where are the emergency phone numbers and supplies?
- ♥ Where is the house key? If there is a home alarm, get details on how to use it.
- ♥ When is bedtime? How long does it take to get ready for bed?

- ♥ Can the children have friends come over to play? Can older children leave and visit friends in their homes?
- ♥ Should you prepare a meal or snack? If so, what foods and drinks?
- ♥ Can you take the children outside or go for a walk (if time appropriate)?
- ♥ What special activities, like reading a story, should you do with the children at bedtime?
- ♥ Are there any off-limit areas or specific do's and don'ts?
- ♥ Ask the parents what you should do if a child refuses to obey or has a tantrum.

Bye-bye time

A small infant or child may cry when the parents leave. This is normal, so don't be alarmed or take it personally. When the parents leave you should:

1 Wave bye-bye with the children at the window or doorway. Make sure they stay away from the moving car.

2 Try to distract the child by playing a game or moving them to another room. Stay with the child and give them tender loving care (TLC).

3 Rock and hold infants as much as needed.

4 Read a book, play a puzzle or go for a walk if you have permission.

5 Lock all the doors and exits after the parents leave.

6 Check all window locks and close the drapes or shades.

7 During evening hours leave outside lights on.

On your own

You're being paid for a job, so give your full attention to the kids! Now is your time to be with the children and get to know them. Talk with the children; find out as much as you can about them and what they like to do. Be a good listener, and try to do things that will involve all the children in your care.

Don't ignore the children by reading your own personal book, watching TV (when they are somewhere else) or doing your homework, unless the children are asleep. Your job is to be with the children. Always know where they are and what they're doing. Remove potential hazards. Check on the children frequently, especially if two or more of them are in different areas of the home. While they are asleep, check on them at least every 15-20 minutes, especially if you're caring for an infant.

Don't eat food unless you have been given permission. Clean up messes made by the children, and let them help whenever possible. Be sure the house is tidy when the parents get home.

Remember, this is a job, and you are being paid to take care of the children. Discourage your friends from calling or visiting unless previously approved by the parents. Absolutely no alcohol, drugs, smoking or abusive behavior is allowed!

Try to choose games or activities based on the ages of the children and be flexible when it comes to game rules. If play becomes too loud or active, try to change the tone. Going for a walk to get out the wiggles, exercising, or looking for a quiet activity such as reading a book or doing a puzzle can help calm them down.

Don't snoop through other people's bedrooms, belongings, private areas, desks or work areas. If you need to find something, contact the parents or a friendly neighbor.

If you become ill on the job, contact the children's parents, your parents or the nearest neighbor. **NEVER leave the children unattended**.

Phone messages

Ask the parents if you should answer the phone during the sit. Sometimes parents leave recorders on so you won't have to be bothered while watching the children.

If the telephone rings while you're babysitting answer it politely. You might say, "Hello, Jones residence." Say that Mrs. Jones is not available right now but that you'd be happy to take a message. For security reasons, never say the parents aren't home or provide any additional information—no matter who is on the phone. In some rare cases, strangers may pretend to be a relative or family friend to get information from you. Always be on your guard.

If you answer the phone, be prepared to take a complete message. Write down the person's full name, the time they called, and their phone number. Ask for the correct spelling of their name. Then leave the note in a place where you won't forget to give it to the parents when they get home. Write telephone messages on the "While You Were Away Form" located in the back of this book.

If you receive a prank or abusive phone call, just hang up! Then let someone close to you know about it. Don't hesitate to let police know if the caller bothers you.

Look what we did!

Parents really want to know how things went during your time with their children. Try to write down things that happened during the sit as they happen so the parents are well informed.

Some important items to note are how the job went, what the children ate, the last time they were fed, when diapers were last changed, any accidents or boo-boos that occurred, and special situations such as tantrums or disagreements. You can put this information on the "While You Were Away Form" located in the back of this book.

TIPS FOR FUN! ----> **Read books**

Children grow and change quickly. Knowing about their stages of growth will help you understand their needs.

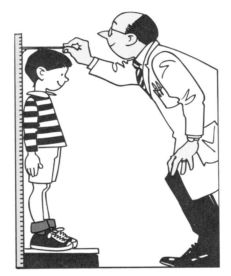

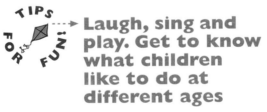

TIPS FOR FUN!

Laugh, sing and play. Get to know what children like to do at different ages

Growing Up–
Fun, Games and Safety

You can have a lot of fun keeping children entertained. First, you'll need to know what children like to do at different ages. If it's been a few months since you last babysat for a family, you may find each child learning and playing at a completely different stage!

Here's a brief description of the stages of growth and development that are common to many children. There is a lot to learn about infants and children, and this is only an introduction. For more information on growth and development, visit your library or talk to the health teacher at your school.

Birth to two months

Infants start their lives in a fragile state. The newborn communicates its needs by crying, and is totally dependent on others for feeding, burping, holding, cuddling, protection, diaper changes, cleanup, warmth and restful times. An infant may sleep as few as six hours a day or as many as 20 hours a day.

The infant requires frequent feedings and diaper changes, so it's very important to get detailed information regarding the location of diapers and accessories, diaper-changing techniques, and perhaps a demonstration of how to make a bottle and feed a baby. When holding an infant, hold the baby close to your body with support to the head, neck and back. Little babies' neck muscles are weak, and their heads will flop if you don't hold them carefully.

Safety
Babysitters should become familiar with the baby equipment and products used in the home such as the crib, changing tables, infant swings, carriers and pacifiers. Accidents can happen through the misuse

of these products, so get instructions from the parents to avoid any hazards.

An infant may roll off high places, such as a changing table, couch or bed, so never leave a baby unattended. If you're bottle feeding, never prop up a bottle as this may lead to choking. Always hold the infant in a well-supported, upright position when feeding. Since small infants spend so much time sleeping, check with the parents for tips on positioning their infant for rest, for instance, on their back or side. When the infant is napping, check on the baby frequently and always respond to crying. Never, ever shake a baby, as this can be very dangerous to them.

Don't panic if a baby cries—it's the baby's only means of communication. Crying can mean all kinds of things. Maybe the baby is lonely, cold, wet, tired, ready for a nap or hungry. Check for all of these things. If there is no obvious problem (such as a diaper pin that has snapped open and is sticking a leg) the baby's diapers are fine, or a bottle is not interesting, then do your best to calm the baby. Try walking around the room holding the baby to your chest, humming a soothing tune and gently rubbing the baby's back. Or try calming the baby by rocking in a rocking chair.

Babies love to be held and they usually respond to your mood if you're affectionate, calm and confident. If nothing seems to work and the baby cries for more than ten minutes, call the parents for advice.

Things to do for fun

New babies sleep a lot. They're so busy getting used to the world that they don't need as much entertaining. They'll be happy if you hold them a little bit, talk or sing in soothing tones, keep them warm, dry, fed, and let them sleep.

Two to six months

At this age babies learn a lot about their new world by touching and tasting. Babies are beginning to grasp all sorts of objects and put them into their mouths. Very soon they'll be able to roll over and move quickly, and become more prone to injury.

These infants are a delight as they make eye contact with you, coo, babble, smile, and try to mimic the sounds you make. They see and hear well, and may look intently at dangling objects. Babies at this age love to be cuddled and crave attention.

Safety

Baby's at this age can roll from side to side and scoot around in their cribs. When placing infants in a crib or playpen make sure the sides are up and properly locked into place to avoid any falls or injuries. Never tie a pacifier around the neck of an infant. Cords and ribbons can twist or catch on a crib and lead to strangulation. Don't hang objects with strings or elastics to a crib or playpen where an infant might become entangled and choke to death.

Infants at this age like to grab at objects, even your hair. Their grip is strong and once they get a hold of something, they can pull with force and sometimes pull things

down on top of them. Be careful about what's in a baby's reach.

Once they have an object, an infant may put it into its mouth and could choke on the item. A baby at this age moves around a lot so NEVER eat, drink or carry anything hot near the baby you're holding as he or she may get burned. Infants from birth to six months are at the highest risk for falls, burns, car injuries, choking or suffocation. Monitor them closely, as they need lots of supervision. Holding, feeding and changing diapers may require practice and if this is your first time, make arrangements to arrive on the job early for advice.

Things to do for fun

Hold and rock them, smile at them and mimic sounds. Sing, shake rattles and play music boxes. Use infant seats and swings when available, making sure to always use safety straps. Talk and read in a soft, gentle voice to infants even though they may not understand. Get down to the baby's level when talking so you don't look like a giant. Go for a walk with a stroller. Play peek-a-boo with your hands. Babies don't need too much entertainment.

Six months to one year

These infants are ACTIVE! They kick, wiggle, and may now be able to crawl, scoot, and pull up to standing positions. Some children learn to walk before their first birthday. They're now able to grab at more objects, and they're very fast and very busy. In fact, they're "on the go" so much of the time that it may be hard to dress and clean them up.

Babies at this age become very attached to their parents, especially their mothers, so they may cry when a new person is introduced.

An infant this age can usually hold its own bottle, and at 10-12 months may drink from a sipper cup. Finger foods may be introduced (check with the parents on which foods are appropriate) so get full details on how meal times are structured and how much they can eat. Babies this age may be teething (which makes them cranky) and they chew on everything. Some are learning simple words like "dada," "mama" and "bye-bye." Talk to them slowly and get down to their level so they can see and hear you.

Safety

Strollers, high chairs, baby walkers, toy boxes and playpens are all potential hazards to infants and toddlers of this age if not properly used. Safety straps are a must in addition to your constant attention. If you use a walker, do not leave the baby unattended, especially near stairs. Throw rugs and carpets can cause a walker to tip over. This active infant may explore by climbing, scooting, crawling or walking and can get stuck in small or narrow spaces. Know where the infant is at all times and be available to help and assist as he or she explores a new world. Any falls should be reported to the parents, so try to write things down as they happen so you won't forget.

When feeding the child, be present during the entire meal. As finger foods are introduced, be alert for signs of choking. During meal preparation keep the child well occupied and to avoid accidents make sure he or she is not under your feet in the kitchen.

Things to do for fun

Read, sing and talk—they may even want to join you. Cuddle. Show them a mirror, since seeing their reflection often fascinates them. Play peek-a-boo or Pat-a-Cake. This age loves repetition and may drop an object over and over for you to pick up. They won't be very interested in television or videos yet, but some babies are very fond of music—just about any variety. Their attention span is not very long at this age, so don't expect them to stay with one activity for more than a few minutes.

Growing Up

One to two years

Toddlers are extremely active and mobile. They seem fearless as they explore their world and are not aware of their limitations. It's up to you to remain close by to keep them safe. There may be lots of dropping, banging and throwing, and you might also receive lots of wet, sticky kisses and hugs. This age also has a hard time separating from their parents.

While many toddlers can say up to three-word sentences, they may still have trouble expressing themselves. They sometimes say "no" when they mean "yes," or may say no to everything. If they have just learned a new word, they will practice it over and over. "Don't touch" and "come here" generally have little effect as they often go in the opposite direction you want. When you want a toddler to come, you may have to go pick them up. Toddlers sometimes experience temper tantrums and can kick and scream for no apparent reason. Be calm, patient and try to ignore the tantrum, as long as you can keep them safe.

Toddlers are now more able to feed themselves, will eat slowly and can be very messy. Have a clean wash cloth nearby. They also have very definite ideas about what they want (or don't want) to eat. Be patient and flexible.

Safety
Just try keeping up with an active toddler! Toddlers need your constant attention as they explore every room of the house. Close doors to off-limit areas such as bathrooms and garages. Toddlers seem to put everything they find into their mouths. If you see a potential hazard such as a small toy, coins, pins, buttons or small batteries in their path, stop and remove it. Be sure to also keep them away from medicines and cleaning agents. Choose toys in good repair to play with and never leave a toddler unattended.

Be sure the play area is safe so the child won't get hurt. Close supervision is a must as lots of falls, bumps and bruises can occur. Always hold hands when crossing the street—no exceptions!

Toddlers can turn on hot water taps and scald themselves. They can also move chairs to get into kitchen cabinets, flush objects down toilets, climb onto counters and turn on appliances. The possibilities for mischief are endless, so keep your eye on them at all times.

Since each toddler is different, ask the parents for guidelines on handling such problems as separation from the parent, meal times, temper tantrums, sharing and how much help the child needs with various tasks.

Things to do for fun
Toddlers love audiences as they play make believe, play with toy telephones, cars, trucks, dolls and building blocks. They may begin working puzzles that have 6-10 pieces. Hearing stories is now a popular pastime, so be prepared to read more than one book. Be aware that they may have a favorite blanket, toy or stuffed animal, and find out what it is. Keep games simple, but be creative. Play games such as hide and seek, or hide yourself or a stuffed animal for the child to find.

The toddler enjoys going on short walks. Be prepared to stop and look at every leaf and stone on the way—that's part of the fun! They enjoy playing with water, sand and mud. They probably have a favorite drawer in the kitchen where they can stack plastic containers and lids or get out wooden spoons. Be sure to keep sharp objects, such as knives, out of their reach. Almost anything can be a toy to a child this age. They're still not ready to watch long television programs, as their attention span is still very short. Toddlers will be happy with your undivided attention.

Two to four years

Two-year-olds are very active and like to do things themselves. The word "no" is often heard as toddlers are busy exploring their world. Try not to give rigid commands, but be sure to provide supervision.

Three-to four-year-olds tend to be more cooperative, and you'll probably hear the word "yes" more often. Some children in this age group have temper tantrums. Find out from the parents how you should cope with these special situations.

Young toddlers in your care will often be making the transition from diapers to the potty. If a young child uses the potty, find out from the parents what the routine is and if they have small a potty-chair or device that fits over the toilet.

Be alert to signs that a small child needs to use the potty, such as tugging at the pants or a hurried movement. Encourage small children to use the bathroom before starting new activities, before going outside, and before or after a meal. Be calm and encouraging—never embarrass a child if there's an accident. Some children will need assistance getting their clothes down or may need help on the toilet. *Don't flush the toilet while they're sitting on it as it may frighten them.*

This age group is learning to do a variety of activities, such as riding tricycles or small bikes. Their attention span is increasing. Many have vivid imaginations and may be fearful and scare easily. Be sensitive to their needs and never scold or embarrass children when they're afraid. Be alert to quarrels over toys and games, especially with brothers or sisters.

Safety

Two to four-year-olds are at risk for injuries from falls, poisons, burns and car accidents. They don't understand what is dangerous, often forget instructions and can't remember "no." This age group can now jump, run and climb with lightening speed, so they need good supervision.

Things to do for fun

Kids of this age like to play with you. They enjoy games like house, ball, store and school, along with simple board games. Explain the rules and be flexible, as this age often doesn't like to lose. They like working with coloring books, clay, blunt scissors, tape, toy dishes, toy animals, books, and enjoy music and singing. In good weather, take them for a walk outdoors. Look for pinecones, leaves, interesting bugs, worms and other nature items. Children this age are so busy playing they'll most likely show you what they want to do.

Five to seven years

Five to seven-year-olds have many accomplishments. These children are attending school and learning to do many things for themselves. As they become more independent, let them discover and learn through new experiences, but remember that they still don't have the judgment to be safe. *Since they rely on you for protection and accident prevention, they'll need gentle reminders about the rules of home, car, fire, water, bike and street safety.*

Most often these children are very agreeable and eager to please. Whenever possible, let them assist you with activities, such as helping with the dishes, lunch or cleanup. They're now able to entertain you with silly stories, new songs and jokes and

some will be eager to read to you. They're continuing to learn new skills and can now hop, skip, jump, somersault and enjoy a variety of outdoor activities. At this age, children will often break the rules just to see if they can get away with it as a way of testing grown ups and babysitters. Follow the parents' rules and be consistent. It will make your job easier, and it helps the children learn to trust you.

Safety

Encourage safety with bicycles, skates, skateboards and other play equipment. Make sure the children are dressed for outdoor weather and use bike helmets and safety equipment where applicable. Know where the children are at all times and who they can play with. Be available to supervise.

Things to do for fun

Make lunch together, work on a craft project, write a story, make up a play, read books, do puzzles, build a tent, play board or card games. They enjoy music and might like to dance or play games like musical chairs. Often they have favorite games they've learned at school that they'd like to share with you.

TIPS FOR FUN! Play Hide-n-Seek or "Follow the Leader"

Eight to ten years

Children eight to ten years of age are really taking off with increased growth and responsibility. They may not like the idea of having a babysitter that is close to their age. Friends are very important to them, and they might want to have a friend over while you're there. They may also try to test your authority. Be kind, considerate and available to meet their needs. Listen to them when they talk to you. Have them do as much for themselves as they can.

Children in the late elementary years are very smart. They might tell you that their parents "made a mistake" about bedtime being 8:00 p.m.—and try to convince you that they "always" go to bed at 10:00 p.m.! Sometimes it's helpful for parents to go over household rules while the children are present so there's no "confusion."

Safety

Remember they are still at risk for accidents. They still need gentle reminders for street, bike, water, fire, car, personal and home safety. Discourage rough play that can result in injuries.

Things to do for fun

Get kids involved in choosing a play activity. They might enjoy sharing some of your favorite movies, activities and games. Talk to the parents ahead of time to learn some of their interests.

TIPS FOR FUN! Play music. Teach new dances.

Be creative during playtime and look for activities that can involve all children.

TIPS FOR FUN! → Have a treasure hunt

Won't You Play With Me?

Be creative during playtime

Who were the babysitters you liked best as a child? Most likely they were the ones who got down on the floor, rolled up their sleeves and really played with you.

Be creative during playtime and look for activities that can involve children of all ages such as singing songs, reading stories, listening to music, working puzzles or playing games. You may have some of your own favorite books or games you enjoyed as a child that you could bring to your jobs.

Check with the parents if you plan to do craft projects or play special games. Always clean up after the project is finished, too. Projects and games should be appropriate for the children's ages. Whatever activity you do, safety is the number one priority. Avoid rough play whenever possible. And remember: **Be flexible!** You may have to adapt games or projects to avoid frustrating smaller children.

Arts and crafts projects can be a lot of fun for both you and the children. Kids love to

create and express themselves through art. Projects don't have to cost a lot of money either. Turn on your imagination and look around your house for potential craft supplies such as recycled envelopes, string, old material, paper, buttons, beads, wrappers, straw, leaves, construction paper, stickers, rubber stamps, crayons and glue.

Remember, in the world of art there are no rights or wrongs—beauty is in the eye of the beholder. Your job as a sitter is to encourage and excite the children about art. Working together, laughing, freedom of expression and enjoying our differences is what arts and crafts are all about. Try to use safe and simple craft projects for younger children who may take more time and need extra supervision. Plan ahead so the children will have enough time to finish a project.

TIPS FOR FUN ----> **Got scrap paper? Make a paper airplane**

Craft ideas for children

This card's for you!

Help the children make a card for someone they love. There doesn't have to be a theme, just have fun! Create thank you cards, birthday cards, or "I love you" cards. Parents like to receive notes from their children!

Supplies:
- ♥ Construction paper
- ♥ Water soluble markers or crayons
- ♥ Stickers
- ♥ Old magazines (to cut out pictures for your card)
- ♥ Glue
- ♥ Scissors

Let your imagination run wild to create fun cards with the kids. You can make the envelopes too.

Edible necklace

Kids will have lots of fun enjoying this tasty snack.

Supplies:
- ✳ Clean string,
- ✳ Round breakfast cereal with a hole in the middle (Cheerios, Fruit Loops)

Cut string long, at least 24 inches. Tie a knot or toothpick to one end to keep cereal from falling off string. Mix and match or use all the same cereal to create an edible, yummy necklace! Tie loosely around neck. Remember to take off necklace during playtime or naps.

Peanut butter bird feeder

This is a great way to have some fun and keep the birds happy.

Supplies:
- ❀ Pinecone
- ❀ Creamy peanut butter
- ❀ Wild birdseed spread out on a dish
- ❀ Yarn: 12-24-inch lengths
- ❀ Wax paper

Find a safe work area and cover with a tablecloth. Work on a sheet of wax paper. Take a pinecone and tie a piece of yarn around the top. Spread peanut butter on each "leaf." Coat liberally. When finished, roll the pinecone in a dish of birdseed. Tie to a tree and watch the birds enjoy themselves. Can wrap cone in waxed paper if saving for a gift.

Cat mask

It doesn't need to be Halloween to have fun making a colorful cat mask.

Supplies:
- Tissue paper
- Construction paper (colored)
- Stickers such as colorful dots or stars
- Cardboard
- Pipe cleaners or soda straws
- Large rubber band
- Glue/tape
- Scissors

Draw a cat face and cut it out of cardboard. Cut eyes about 2-1/2 inches apart. On separate sheets of tissue paper, draw fringe in two colors for eyelashes and cut out. Cut out a cat nose and use pipe cleaners or straws for whiskers. Glue to mask. Use stickers for additional decoration. Cut rubber band and attach ends to sides of mask with tape to hold it onto the child's ears.

Homemade play dough (No-cook recipe)

Kids will enjoy making this dough recipe with you, but check with the parents ahead of time about the details and supplies. You can make this recipe at home and bring it to your sit, too!

Mix in separate bowl:
- 1/2 cup salt
- 1 cup white flour
- 2 Tbsp. vegetable oil
- 1 tsp. alum (if you can't find it at the grocery store, it is available at the drugstore)

Blend together the following ingredients and slowly add to flour mixture.
- 1/2 cup warm water
- 1 pkg. unsweetened Kool-Aid (provides color and a nice smell)

Slowly mix liquid with flour until it's the consistency of bread dough. You may not need to add all the Kool-Aid/water mixture. Store in an airtight container or plastic bag. Dough will last a long time. Use in the kitchen so it won't get it into the carpet.

Won't You Play with Me?

A-maze the kids

Make copies of the maze so you can have fun with it again & again.

Help!

*Baby needs a new diaper and it's time for all the children to get ready for bed. Help the sitter locate children and pets first. Then go to the center once you have located everyone. (**Hint:** As you gather the kids and pets you may need to re-trace your steps.)*

Start

Other suggested games:

Finger/hand games:
Pat-a-Cake (infants)
Peek-a-Boo (infants)
Itsy Bitsy Spider (singing too)

Board games:
Candyland (3-6 years)
Checkers (6-10 years)
Life, Monopoly (7 years and up)
Animal Bingo

Puzzles:
4-6 pieces (For toddlers, puzzles with knobs are easier)
10-25 pieces (3-5 years)
50-100 pieces (4-8 years)
200 + pieces (8 years and up)

Outdoor games:
Simon Says
Red Light–Green Light
Hide the Flag

Cards:
Go Fish
Animal Rummy
Old Maid
Concentration

If you're planning active games that involve running or going outdoors, check to see if anyone needs to use the bathroom before going outside to avoid "accidents." Be sure to clean up after each game or project before going on to something else. Have the children help—you can even make a game out of it.

Choosing safe toys

Be careful when selecting toys for children to play with. Just because they're lying around the house doesn't mean they're safe or appropriate. Read labels. Look for and pay attention to age recommendations. For example, if a toy says "not recommended for children under three," put it away from young toddlers.

Infant toys, such as rattles, squeeze toys and teethers, should be large enough so they can't become stuck in a baby's throat. Even balloons, when uninflated or broken, can choke or suffocate very young children who try to swallow them.

Check toys for breakage. Take away broken or damaged toys, or objects that you feel

could be dangerous. This includes toys with sharp edges, small parts, pointed objects, toys that make a loud noise, or toys with strings that could entangle infants or small children. Look out for projectiles like guided missiles or darts and other flying toys that could injure children's eyes. Electric toys should be used only by children old enough to handle them properly. Supervise carefully if children are using electric toys.

TIPS FOR SAFETY --→ **Monitor small items that young children may put in their mouths**

For safety, don't allow children to get underfoot while you're cooking.

TIPS FOR FUN! → **Invent a new snack**

Food, Glorious Food!

Get complete instructions

Learning how to prepare properly cooked foods is an essential skill that will benefit you for a lifetime. If you haven't done much cooking before, ask your parents for instructions and cooking tips before you prepare meals in another person's home. Becoming a good cook takes time and practice, but you could be cooking tasty meals for others before you know it.

Before cooking in another person's home, get clear, detailed instructions on how to use their appliances and find out where supplies are located in their kitchen. Find out what, when and where the children should eat. Also ask where the kitchen fire extinguisher is located and how to use it.

If you are asked to prepare a meal and you don't feel comfortable cooking or working the appliances, don't be afraid to tell the parents. There are lots of simple meals you can prepare that require no cooking at all.

Here are some basic kitchen safety rules (to discuss with your parents), cooking tips and easy-to-follow recipes to try at home. Have a fun, safe time while you learn to cook!

Kitchen safety rules

1 Before handling food, wash your hands with soap and hot water. You may need to wash your hands several times during and after food preparation.

2 If you'll be using the stove, first clear the area of any potential fire hazards such as cookbooks or recipes, dishtowels and paper products. Also be sure to tie your hair back, remove loose clothing and roll up your sleeves since these also could catch fire.

3 Make sure no one is under foot when moving hot liquid. Never hold hot liquids and infants or small children at the same time.

4 Clean up messes and spills as you go to avoid falls and contamination of other surfaces.

5 Always turn pot handles on the stove or counter inward so children can't bump or grab them, causing hot liquids to spill.

6 Never leave food you're cooking unattended.

7 Don't use appliances with frayed or damaged cords.

8 Never put anything into a microwave unless you're absolutely sure it's safe. For example, metal is not safe to microwave.

9 Cool all foods sufficiently before serving to children.

10 Never pour water onto grease or cooking fires. It could splatter and burn you. Put a tight fitting lid or cookie sheet over the top of the pot or use the kitchen fire extinguisher or baking soda to smother the flames.

11 **If you're unable to put the fire out right away, leave the house with the children and call the fire department from a neighbor's house.**

12 Always use a dry potholder or oven mitt when handling hot pots and pans.

13 When adding food to boiling water, add gently to avoid splashing hot fluid on yourself. Using a hot-pan holder, lift lids from boiling pots with the opening away from you so the steam doesn't burn you.

14 When using a sharp knife, pick it up by the handle and cut away from your body. Place sharp objects away from counter edges. Always clean and return knives to their proper area after use.

15 When finished cooking, turn off all stove and oven dials, clean up all messes, and wash your hands.

Helpful hints to get you started in food preparation

✦ Always check with a parent before using their kitchen.
✦ Have a meal plan or study a recipe, then assemble all ingredients.
✦ Make sure the food preparation area is clean and uncluttered. Gather everything you need before you begin cooking. Wash your hands with soap and hot water.
✦ Wear an apron to protect your clothing.
✦ Wash fresh foods with water before cutting or eating.
✦ Keep food items stored at the proper temperature. Keep foods, such as eggs, meats, sauces and milk, refrigerated to avoid spoilage.
✦ For best results, follow a recipe exactly.
✦ Use a timer to remind you when cooking time is up.
✦ When in doubt, ask questions or call your parent for help.
✦ Don't forget to clean up.

Simple foods are best

Ask the parents what foods are appropriate for their children. Be careful not to give small children foods that will be hard to eat or that they might choke on. Children also need something to drink, such as milk and juice, with their meal. Some good, simple snack foods for children are:

➤ fruits
➤ cheese
➤ milk
➤ hard-boiled eggs
➤ finger sandwiches

➤ fruit juices
➤ crackers
➤ yogurt
➤ dry cereal
➤ peanut butter on bread or crackers

Food, Glorious Food!

Mealtime

Before serving the meal, encourage children to sit down. Put the little ones in a high chair where you can watch them, but they're not in your way. Let older kids can entertain themselves at the kitchen table, for example, with coloring books, or they can help you set the table.

Mealtime isn't the time for games and distractions. **Stay with the children while they eat in case problems, such as choking, arise.** Small pieces of foods are easiest to chew and swallow. Select foods that are the right texture and size. If you're not sure about a certain food, don't use it and check with the parents later. Be patient with infants and small children— they can be very slow and messy eaters. Be sure to clean up after mealtime is over.

Infant feeding tips

♥ Get tips from the parents about feeding infants, as parents often want the baby fed in specific way. Also, babies at different stages have different needs and capabilities. Don't force feed. Be patient, and have fun getting to know the infant.

♥ Ask parents how they'd like you to prepare and heat bottles for their baby, even if you've fixed bottles for other babies before.

♥ In general, don't microwave breast milk or formula. Microwaving can cause uneven temperatures in the bottle, causing a baby's mouth or throat to burn.

♥ Never give honey to an infant under 1-year to avoid infant botulism.

♥ Cover and refrigerate leftover baby food.

♥ Use a cloth to clean messy hands and faces after feeding.

Feeding is a social time for the baby, and requires your undivided attention. Always hold a small infant in your arms during a bottle feeding, with the baby's neck supported and head elevated.

To avoid accidental choking, never prop a bottle on a pillow or towel while feeding the baby.

Hold the bottle at about a 45-degree angle. Older babies can often hold their own bottles, or enjoy milk straight out of the refrigerator. Check with the parent first. Burp the baby frequently to release air trapped in the tummy. Young infants usually enjoy a nap after being fed. Ask the parents for tips on positioning their infant after feeding, for instance, on their back or side.

Toddler feeding tips

❀ Serve simple foods in small portions. Don't mix foods.

❀ Even though many can feed themselves, stay at the table while they eat.

❀ Cut large pieces of food into bite-sized pieces for easier chewing and swallowing.

❀ To avoid choking, don't let children walk around with food in their mouths. Make it a rule to only eat food at the table.

❀ Toddlers eat slowly, so don't rush or force feed them.

❀ Be ready to clean up after a toddler, as they can be messy eaters.

Ask the parents for favorite snack ideas and how they are prepared

Find out meal times and how much the children normally eat

Snack ideas

If you babysit a lot, you know that mealtime can sometimes get boring, especially for older children. As you get more confident in your food preparation skills, get creative and invent fun, nutritious snacks. Involve the kids, too!

Below are some ideas to brighten up mealtime. Remember to ask the parents, and not to get too complicated or make too much. *Simple foods really are the best.*

Yummy Yogurt

This is one delicious snack! You may be able to get in the four food groups, too—fruits/veggies, protein, cereals and dairy. Add a topping to any flavor of yogurt and mix and match.

Strawberries	Granola	Sunflower seeds
Raspberries	Brown rice	Rice Krispies
Blueberries	Grapenuts	Walnuts
Bananas	Raisins	Chopped apples
Melon cubes	Dates	Shredded wheat
Orange sections	Apricots	Shredded carrots

Ants on a Log (For ages 4-6)

Kids will love to help fix this fun, healthy snack.

1 The logs can be:

Apple slices	Carrot sticks
Celery sticks	Halved bananas
Bread sticks	

2 Then spread one of the following on the sticks or slices:

Peanut butter	Cream cheese	Processed cheese

3 For ants, roll the coated sticks in your choice of:

Raisins	Chopped nuts
Dates	Chopped apricots
Granola	Chocolate or carob chips

Ice Cream Sandwich

Ice cream sandwiches are fast, easy, and always a big hit!

For each sandwich you'll need:
- Two big cookies of any kind— such as chocolate chip or peanut butter
- One scoop of vanilla, strawberry, or chocolate ice cream
- Sprinkles

Instructions:
Place one scoop of ice cream between two cookies. Handle gently and roll ice cream on plate of sprinkles. Place on small cookie sheet in the freezer for approximately 15–25 minutes.

Ice Cream Floats

You'll need:
- A favorite pop, such as root beer or orange, or juice, and vanilla ice cream.
- Large glasses, ice cream scoop, and stirring spoon.

Instructions:
Fill glasses 2/3 full with beverage and gently add a scoop of vanilla ice cream. Yum!

Bunny Salad

You'll need:
One can of halved pears, cottage cheese, 2-3 slices of American cheese (cut into narrow strips), lettuce leaves, raisins or green olives with pimiento for the eyes, and maraschino cherries for the nose.
Optional: marshmallows for the tail.

Can opener, small knife, cutting board, spoons and small plate for each person

Instructions:
Place lettuce leaf on each plate. Place one scoop of cottage cheese on the lettuce leaf for the bunny's head. Next, place one pear half for the body, below the cottage cheese head. Cut another pear half in two, and place above cottage cheese for ears. Cut American cheese into narrow strips for whiskers (three on each side of face). Place olives or raisins for the eyes. Use a cherry half for the mouth or nose. Use a dab of cottage cheese or marshmallow for the tail.

Salad Toss

You'll need:
Head of iceberg lettuce, 1 cucumber (peeled and sliced) and 1 tomato (diced), bottled salad dressing.
Suggested toppings: bacon bits, cheese, croutons, bell pepper, onion, broccoli, shredded carrots, apples or pears. What else can you think of?

Large bowl, colander, paper towels, cutting board, sharp knife, and tossing forks or spoons.

Instructions:
Rinse the lettuce with cold water and drain in colander. Pat leaves dry with paper towel. Tear leaves into bite-sized pieces. Rinse, peel and slice the cucumber, then cut and slice the tomato. Toss together with the lettuce in a large bowl. Cover and refrigerate. Toss with favorite dressing just before serving.

Food, Glorious Food!

To keep everyone safe, find out the best way to handle the pet.

TIPS FOR SAFETY ---> Don't leave small infants or children alone with family pets

Taking Care of the Family Pet

When you meet a family for the first time, chances are you'll also meet the family pet. And, no matter how lovable Fido or Fluffy may be, they might get a little excited and bite, cut or scratch you or the children.

To help prevent a dog or cat bite or scratch, follow some of these pet safety tips:

▲ Never run up to a dog or cat. Wait for the family to introduce you to their pet.

▲ When meeting a pet for the first time, speak softly, don't act afraid.

▲ Before petting, extend your hand for the pet to see and sniff, then pet gently. Make sure you keep your face away from the animal.

▲ **Be sure to supervise children around pets at all times. Don't leave small infants or children alone with family pets.**

▲ Do not let children grab, pull ears or tails of animals.

▲ Be careful not to play too hard and loud around a family pet as this may get a pet excited and accidentally put the animal in a protect mode, causing the pet to bite.

▲ Never attempt to touch a dog or cat when it is eating or in possession of a special treat.

▲ If at any time the family pet appears to be unfriendly (is not wagging a tail or is growling or showing its teeth or barking), don't attempt to pet it. Move yourself and the children away from the pet and call the parents.

▲ If you feel uncomfortable around pets, tell the parents. They can locate a safe area of the home to keep a pet while you babysit.

▲ **Ask lots of questions about your responsibility for caring for the pet. For instance, if or when pets can go outside, what they eat, where their water dish is located, and whether there are any off-limit areas.**

▲ Ask the parent to include a veterinarian's number with your emergency phone numbers.

Give your full attention to children at bath time.

TIPS FOR SAFETY

An infant or child can drown in just a few inches of water. **NEVER** leave an infant or child alone around any water source, including puddles, buckets, bathtubs, toilets, swimming pools or hot tubs, not even for a second.

Scrub-a-dub-dub

If you're asked to give a child a bath, remember that bathing a small infant or child requires your full attention. If you don't feel capable of bathing infants or young children, be sure to tell the parents ahead of time.

When giving a child a bath, prepare for the bath ahead of time and have everything you need assembled before you put the child into the water. Under the right circumstances, bathing can be a lot of fun for both you and the child. To get ready, follow the bath-time checklist below. You may want to show the parent this list. Write down any special instructions or helpful hints the parents might have.

Bath-time checklist:

- ❑ Run warm water in the tub. Find out how much before the parents leave.
- ❑ Bring in the child's underwear and clothes or pajamas.
- ❑ Arrange soap, towels and washcloth near the tub.
- ❑ **Remove any electrical appliances around the tub, such as hair dryers, electric razors or toothbrushes.**
- ❑ Test the water temperature on your wrist. It should feel pleasantly warm but not too hot.
- ❑ Help the child into the bathtub.
- ❑ Assist the child, depending on age, with a head-to-toe scrub. Watch out for soap in the eyes.
- ❑ Supervise the child at play. No jumping allowed.
- ❑ **If the doorbell or phone rings, do NOT answer. Do not leave the child unattended. Whoever it is will call back.**
- ❑ Towel dry the child thoroughly after the bath and help with getting dressed. Wipe up any spills outside the tub to avoid a fall as you leave the bathroom. Empty the tub before you leave.
- ❑ After the child is dry and dressed, walk back into the bathroom and look around. Is it clean? Is all the water out of the tub? Put away towels and dirty clothes.

Hot

Warm

Cold

NEVER leave an infant or child alone in water, even for a moment!
If left unsupervised for even a few seconds they could drown in just a few inches of water.

With practice,
changing a diaper
will become easy
for you and the baby
will enjoy being
comfortable and dry.

TIPS FOR FUN! ---> Sing soothing songs while changing a diaper

Due for a Change

Do you panic at the mention of the D-word—diaper? Do you cross your fingers and hope the baby won't wet all afternoon? Well, don't worry. Changing diapers isn't hard, and it really doesn't take a cast-iron stomach either. With a little practice you'll quickly become a pro and the children you take care of will be much more comfortable with frequent, efficient changes. If you've never changed a diaper, ask your parents to show you how. Try to arrange some time with a mother in your neighborhood so you can practice on her young children.

To change a diaper:

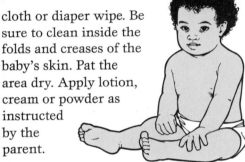

- ✿ You will need to lay a gentle hand on the baby because who may wiggle and squirm during a change. Be alert; prevent falls from high surfaces. Never leave infants unattended during changes.

- ✿ Find out where diapers, supplies and extra clothing are located.

- ✿ Find out what kind of diaper they use. It will either be a disposable diaper (which comes with its own stick-on tabs) or a cloth diaper (which is used with protective plastic pants and safety pins).

- ✿ Ask what their usual procedure is and what they use to clean the baby's bottom. Some people use pre-moistened wipes. Others use a wet washcloth.

- ✿ *Assemble all supplies before beginning. Before removing the soiled diaper, have the cleaning supplies and new diaper ready to go as babies wiggle and squirm during changes.*

- ✿ Remove the soiled diaper by first unpinning or removing the tapes. Lift the baby by gently grasping the ankles of both legs and lifting the legs and hips to remove the soiled diaper. Wash the diaper area thoroughly with a damp

cloth or diaper wipe. Be sure to clean inside the folds and creases of the baby's skin. Pat the area dry. Apply lotion, cream or powder as instructed by the parent.

- ✿ Lift the legs and bottom again and place the clean diaper underneath the baby's bottom.

- ✿ Pull the diaper between the legs and tape or pin each side.

- ✿ **If you're using a cloth diaper with pins, place your finger between the diaper and the baby when pinning. It is better to poke your finger instead of the baby. Be sure to keep pins closed and out of the baby's reach.**

- ✿ If using cloth diapers, put on the baby's plastic pants. Use clean ones if the original pants are either wet or dirty.

- ✿ Dispose of dirty diapers according to the parents' instructions.

Arrange quiet activities, such as coloring or reading, right before bedtime to help the children wind down.

TIPS FOR FUN! → Read a bedtime story

Sweet Dreams

"Bedtime" is not the most welcome word to children—it often brings tears and tantrums. Here are some tips to help bedtime go a little smoother.

Bedtime tips

Zzz Find out from the parents the time for bed and the children's routine.

Zzz Try to follow the child's regular routine as closely as possible. It's good to know if the child has a special blanket or stuffed animal, or if he or she uses a pacifier.

Zzz When you announce bedtime, be friendly but firm.

Zzz Try to arrange quiet activities right before bedtime, such as coloring, reading or watching TV. This helps the child "wind down."

Zzz Let the children know about 30 minutes ahead that bedtime is coming. Suggest they use the time to get comfortable in their pajamas and brush their teeth, so you can read a story.

Zzz Make sure the children are in bed and ready for sleep at the time suggested by the parents. With infants, be sure to ask the parent how you should position the baby, for example, on the back or the side.

Zzz Once bedtime has arrived, go with the children and tuck them in bed. Read a story or two. Leave a night light or hall light on and be nearby for any problems that might occur.

Zzz If you're watching TV or listening to the radio, keep the volume low so as not to disturb sleeping children.

Zzz Check on sleeping children every 20 to 30 minutes.

Zzz Try to stay awake while you're babysitting. If you know the parents will be very late, discuss your sleeping time with them and locate a suitable area near the children so you can be available in case someone needs you.

Keep your care simple and be supportive. Remember lots of TLC: tender, loving care. Keep your care simple and be supportive. Remember lots of TLC: tender, loving care.

Simple things are best!

Once you determine what has caused a child's crying, do something simple to make things better. A bandage, kiss, holding, cuddling, or rocking may be just the right medicine to calm the child down if the situation seems minor. When simple interventions don't help to calm a crying infant or child call a parent for advice.

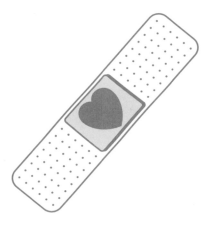

TIPS FOR SAFETY

When in doubt call the parents, your parents or 911 for advice

Remember lots of TLC: tender, loving care. Keep your care simple and be supportive. Remember lots of TLC: tender, loving care. Keep your care simple and be supportive. Remember lots of TLC: tender, loving care. Keep your care simple and be supportive. Remember lots of TLC: tender, loving care. Keep your care simple and be

What's Wrong?

If you involve yourself with the children's activities and take the time to be with them, they'll usually be happy and content. Sometimes children cry, especially if they're afraid, ill, angry or hurt. Crying is a signal that someone needs your immediate and supportive attention. As a babysitter, part of your job will be to go to a crying infant or child and find out what's wrong, which is not always easy.

Temper tantrums

Sometimes crying is the result of a fit of bad temper or frustration, otherwise known as a temper tantrum. These tantrums are more likely to occur when a child is tired, is not getting his or her way, or is in need of attention. While it's not always understandable why some kids have temper tantrums, which can include kicking, screaming, yelling, and hitting in addition to crying, it is clear that physical punishment is not the solution.

Never shake, spank or verbally abuse a child in your care, for any reason. When children experience a tantrum, your goal will be to keep them from harming themselves or others. Ask the parents for more information on how they handle this situation. Try distracting the child with a game, toy or favorite activity, which helps the child forget what caused the tantrum. Some parents use time out, which separates the child from the rest of the family for a short period of time, so he or she can calm down. It is important to get good guidelines from the parents before implementing time outs.

After a tantrum is over, take note of it and let the parents know about it. Try to talk it over with the child, if they're old enough, and discuss what happened calmly and with love.

What should I do?

A crying infant or child needs immediate and supportive attention. Your approach should be calm and gentle. **Give lots of TLC—that's Tender, Loving, Care.** Try to calm down the child and provide assurance that you're there to answer any questions and to explain what's going on.

If you suspect an injury, keep the child from moving so that any injuries will not be made worse. Take note of what you see and go on an "Owie Hunt" to look over their body for other injuries. Look them over from head to toe, including the mouth, to make sure you haven't missed anything. It takes less than a minute to do this hunt.

How to decide if you need to call the parents or your parents for advice:

☞ When you have questions about the family routine.

☞ When visitors show up unannounced.

☞ When you receive prank phone calls.

☞ When you can't resolve the children's fights.

☞ If you suspect a child is ill.

☞ If you don't feel safe.

☞ When you have questions about home appliances or products.

☞ When a child is injured.

☞ When simple interventions don't help to calm a crying infant or child.

☞ When you feel sick and are unable to care for the children.

☞ Basically whenever you have doubts or questions.

Better Safe Than Sorry

Most of the time during your babysitting jobs everything will go smoothly. But the reason parents hired you is to have someone responsible looking after their children—just in case something does go wrong.

Calling for emergency help (911 in most areas)

The most important thing about any emergency is that you don't have to handle it alone! Help is just a phone call away. Don't feel that you have to be brave. Instead, pick up the telephone and call for emergency medical help (911 in most areas). The operators who answer are trained to handle all kinds of problems such as fires, police calls and medical emergencies. They'll ask you a few questions, so take a big breath and answer as calmly as you can.

Note about 911: **In many areas across the United States the emergency number is 911. But that is not true in all areas. Be sure to find out the emergency number where you babysit.**

When you make a call for emergency help be ready to provide clear and accurate information:

1 State that this is an emergency and that you need advice or help immediately.

2 Let the operator know you're the babysitter and give your name.

3 Give the parents' names.

4 Verify the address and nearest cross street to where the situation is happening.

5 Explain the circumstances and follow their advice.

6 Stay on the line until they tell you to hang up.

Calling the parents or your own parents

You can—and should—also call the parents you're babysitting for, especially if things are getting out of control but you don't think you need the police, ambulance or fire department. Maybe the two-year-old child just won't stop crying. Maybe two older children are fighting, and you can't get them to calm down. Perhaps a child has developed a high fever. Don't feel bad about "bothering" the parents. If you've tried your best to handle a situation without success, pick up the phone.

You can also call your own parents if you're puzzled about how to handle a situation. Or, sometimes people will leave phone numbers of trusted neighbors or friends who can help you. Don't be bashful. Give these people a call when you need help.

In a power failure

☞ If the power goes out, call out to the children to locate and reassure them.

☞ Look for flashlights and gather the children in a safe area of the home. Most power failures don't last too long so fill the time with stories and songs.

☞ Gather blankets, drinks and snack items as you wait for further instructions.

☞ Contact the parents of the children or your parents if the phone is working. Limit your time on the telephone except for emergency use. Avoid using the phone during lightning and thunderstorms.

☞ Never leave the children unattended. If you have to move, always stay together.

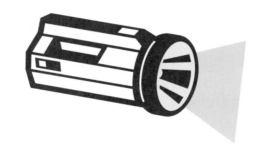

Home Security

The best protection against danger is knowing how to avoid it. Sometimes you only get seconds to make good decisions regarding the family's personal safety. Take the time to learn about how to protect yourself and the children from harm because bad situations can present themselves day or night. You will want to know a lot about handling serious situations before you go on the job. Below are some tips that will hopefully lead to discussion with you and your parents about making good decisions when a problem presents itself.

Never open the door to strangers and never tell anyone who comes to the door that you're alone. A person may identify themselves as a friend, neighbor, or relative and request to come in, but unless you have instructions from the parents to do so you may be placing yourself and the children in harm. Tell the person at the door that you are visiting, the parent is busy and unable to come to the door. Tell him or her to come back later.

If a person hangs around, or tries to get in, don't hesitate to call the police (911).

If you answer the phone NEVER say you're alone. Again, say you are visiting, the parent(s) can't come to the phone right now, but you'll give them a message. If anyone persists or gets angry, just hang up. If you receive a crank phone call, hang up. Don't be afraid to call the police or your parents and tell them about the call. Many homes have answering machines that will allow you to screen calls before you answer. Don't leave the phone off the hook, as a parent may call to check how the evening is going and become concerned when their call doesn't go through.

Who turned off the lights?

As a babysitter, the most likely sudden situation you'll usually have to deal with is a "Power Outage." When the unexpected happens, act calmly and responsibly—the children depend on you to stay calm and make good decisions. Moving in the dark requires some fine tuning, so move slowly until your eyes have had time to adjust.

Safety tips:

✢ If an unexpected situation occurs, stay calm! Take a few seconds to think about what's happening and what to do next. Gather the children and give them instructions on what to do. They will need your calm reassurance.

✢ During bad storms, stay off the phone. If power lines are damaged, your home is flooded or lightning is present, it could be a fatal mistake.

Know what to do should an earthquake occur.

✣ Inside the house during an earthquake, DROP under something heavy, and COVER your head. HOLD onto the furniture you have ducked under. STAY INSIDE.

✣ Outside during an earthquake, MOVE into the open, away from buildings, bridges, power lines, utility poles, and trees. DROP to the ground. STAY in the open until the shaking stops.

TIPS FOR SAFETY

- - -> **In unstable weather areas, make sure you have flashlights and a portable radio for information.**

The Great Outdoors

Children love to play outside and explore. As a babysitter there are many situations to consider before going outside, such as the weather and safe areas. Ask the parents for permission before you take children outside.

If you're taking a baby in a stroller, ask the parents to show you how the stroller works. Find out how to open the stroller, and how to set the brake in case you need to stop. Ask how to adjust the back (most strollers allow a baby to either sit or lie down) and find out how the baby usually likes to be positioned. Don't tie a pet to the stroller when walking outdoors. A pet could get distracted and run off with the stroller.

If you take children outside, make sure you have the house key with you before you leave. If the home has an alarm, find out how to secure and disable the alarm. Double-check to be certain all doors and windows are locked. Have the children use the bathroom before you go outside. Leave at least one outside light on during evening hours.

Be especially careful near driveways, roads, swimming pools, garages, unfamiliar pets and wild animals. Know where the children are allowed to play and who they're allowed to play with. Find out from the parents if playmates are okay. If you're unsure about a strange pet you encounter, turn around and walk away to avoid a confrontation.

When crossing streets always hold hands and look both ways before crossing. Cross within the boundaries of crosswalks and obey all traffic rules.

Always supervise children around water. And never leave an infant or child alone around water—not even for a second.

If children are riding bicycles, tricycles or other vehicles, be sure their helmets fit correctly and that they wear the helmet each time they ride— no exceptions. Stay nearby to supervise and find out where they're allowed to ride.

When you're out with the children, don't talk to strangers. If you feel you're being followed, go to a nearby home, store or gas station and call the police immediately.

Hot weather

When the weather is hot and sunny, children need extra protection from the sun. Prevention is the key to avoiding sunburn and heat exhaustion.

Sun safety tips

- ☼ Keep infants out of direct sun, lightly covered in the shade. Encourage fluids. Most sunscreens are not recommended for infants less than 6 months old. Check with the parents.

- ☼ Keep infants and small children out of direct sun contact during peak sun hours (between 10:00 a.m. and 2:00 p.m.) and use cover-ups such as hats or umbrellas to provide shade.

- ☼ Apply an approved sunblock (SPF 15 or greater) provided by the parents at least a half-hour before going outdoors. Ask parents if the sunscreen should be repeated.

- ☼ Don't forget to offer plenty of fluids when kids are out in the sunshine, especially juices and water. Popsicles are great outdoor thirst quenchers and fun to make too.

- ☼ Dress children according to the weather, usually light colored, lightweight clothing. If you're not sure about the right clothing, ask the parents before they leave.

- ☼ On hot days, encourage the children to play in the shade.

- ☼ Don't push heavy meals during hot weather; children usually do better with small frequent meals.

Cold weather

There are three important factors to consider when going out in cold weather—wind, humidity and temperature. Young children can lose heat quickly in bad weather to these conditions. Ice and wet surfaces can also make areas slippery and cause some bad falls. It is your job to supervise and make good judgment about going outside in cold weather. If you're not sure, call the parents or your parents for advice. If you must go outside be sure to dress for the weather and follow these safety tips.

Cold weather safety tips

❄ Be prepared to go outside with the children.

❄ During cold weather, have the children dress in layers.

❄ Prevent heat loss from the body by having the children put on gloves, a hat and waterproof jacket.

❄ Have children wear waterproof boots with good traction.

❄ If clothing or shoes gets wet, change into warm clothes and dry shoes right away.

❄ Watch for signs of cold stress such as irritability, fatigue, shivering and tingling nose, ear lobes, fingers and toes. Be sure to bring the children inside for a warm-up if any of these conditions exist.

❄ In addition to warm clothing, heat children up with soups and beverages. Avoid caffeine products.

The Great Outdoors

Tips for preventing fires:

➤ Good housekeeping—decrease clutter, rubbish and blocked escape routes.

➤ Keep any matches and lighters out of sight and reach.

➤ Do not overload electrical outlets.

➤ Tell the parents if you find any frayed cords or broken plugs so they can be replaced.

➤ Keep appliances clean and in good repair. When not in use, unplug appliances.

➤ Note the location of fire extinguishers and smoke detectors.

If a fire occurs, get everyone outside immediately! Have a designated meeting spot so you can count heads.

Fire Safety

Get fired up about safety!

It's important to learn about fire safety and be aware of dangers while you babysit. Each year home fires kill more than 6,000 people, injure over 200,000 and destroy millions of dollars in property in the United States.

Preparation will help you prevent fires and make good decisions if a fire occurs.

Detection

Many fatal fires occur in homes at night while the family is sleeping. But they can happen any time of day or night. Smoke detectors can alert people while the fire is still small and give them enough time to get out of the house. Smoke detectors can run by battery or electricity, and work well if maintained and are properly tested. Talk to the parents about the number and locations of their smoke detectors.

Escape

Learn the family's fire escape plan so you'll know the best ways out of the house. Have an assigned meeting place to gather outside if a fire occurs.

Remind the children that in case of fire, they need to keep low, hold hands, and crawl out on their hands and knees. If someone's clothes catch on fire remember to **"Stop! Drop! And Roll!"** To keep them from burning, smother the flames with a blanket.

If a fire occurs, get everyone outside immediately!
If you're in the middle of getting the children ready for bed or bathing them, don't stop to get them dressed or try to put out the fire. Many deaths occur from smoke inhalation since smoke and fumes can kill in minutes, so get out fast!
Once out, stay out, and call the fire department (911) from a neighbor's house or nearby phone immediately.

Be alert to signs of illness while you are on the job.

TIPS FOR SAFETY ---→ To prevent the spread of germs to you or the child, wash your hands frequently, especially if working with dirty wounds or sick children.

Illness

Since young children seem to be prone to colds and illnesses, especially during the fall and winter months, you need to be alert to the signs of illness while you are on the job. Signs of illness can include runny nose, irritability, excessive crying, fever, cramps, diarrhea, vomiting, nausea, headache, muscle aches and pains, rashes, thick greenish/gray nasal secretions, coughs, sore throat, drowsiness, loss of appetite, decrease in fluids taken, earache, and a general feeling of weakness.

Action: *Contact parents.*

♦ Have the child rest in a safe, comfortable area.

♦ Ask the child what is wrong and where it hurts or feels bad.

♦ Contact the parents and give them the details. Stay nearby and be supportive.

♦ Since the child's appetite may be poor, do not force the child to eat.

♦ Slowly offer small frequent sips of fluids like water or juice.

♦ Continue to reassure the child until the parents come home.

♦ When you can't contact the parents, call your own parents or a contact from your list of emergency numbers.

♦ **IMPORTANT!**
Never give or apply medicine to a child unless you have clear written instructions from the parents. These instructions should include: 1) the name of child, 2) exact name of medicine, 3) correct amount to give, 4) how often the medicine should be given, 5) name of doctor and phone number (if prescription), and 6) helpful ways to get the child to take the medicine.

Safety tip:

To avoid the spread of contagious illness, encourage a child to cover his or her mouth when coughing and to wash his or her hands frequently. You should wash your hands frequently especially when caring for sick children, cleaning wounds, wiping noses, using the bathroom, changing diapers and preparing food.

Coughs, sneezes and sore throats

We all cough and sneeze from time to time to keep our breathing passages free and clear. However, when a child's cough worsens or they complain of a worsening sore throat, you should consider these symptoms as a sign of illness.

Most minor coughs or sore throats require very little intervention. You can help make the child feel better by offering gentle support and cool liquids or Popsicles to soothe a sore throat.

Serious Coughs

If a child can't stop coughing, has a fever with a cough or you begin to notice a barking, croaking cough, you need to contact the parents or get medical advice. This kind of cough could lead to difficulty in breathing.

Action: *Contact parents or 911.*

- Have the child rest.
- When coughing is hard, a child will often feel more comfortable sitting up.
- You can sometimes quiet a cough with water, juices, or Popsicles.
- Cooling the child's breathing passages often improves a barky cough. You may be advised to have the child breath moist air in a steamy bathroom or to bundle the child up and go outside in the cool night air.
- Stay with the child and provide tender, loving support. Wash your hands frequently.
- Ask the parent to come home if the child exhibits worsening symptoms.
- Call 911 if skin is bluish or child has difficulty breathing.

Diarrhea and vomiting

Diarrhea and vomiting can be scary, embarrassing and tiring to young children, so be very supportive. Diarrhea (frequent, watery stools) and vomiting can have the same warning signs such as stomach pain, stomach cramps, loss of appetite, or nausea. Most cases are brief and without complications.

Children, especially infants, lose a lot of fluids from the body whenever they experience diarrhea or vomiting. Your goal as a babysitter is to keep the child as comfortable as possible, assist the child

during periods of diarrhea and vomiting, slowly replace lost fluids, prevent the spread of germs by good handwashing, and to notify the parents for advice, especially if taking care of an infant.

Action: *Contact parents.*

For diarrhea:

♦ Stay with the child and reassure him or her. Count the numbers of stools and frequency. Call the parents, especially if you are watching an infant.
♦ Rest the stomach. Children will often not feel like eating so don't push food.
♦ Young children and infants with diarrhea will need to have lost fluids replaced. Get guidelines from the parent or family doctor. *(See safety tip.)*
♦ As you begin to replace foods, avoid milk, citrus juices, spicy or fried foods.
♦ If stomach pain is severe or there's high fever or vomiting, or you are caring for a sick infant, contact a doctor if you can't contact the parents.
♦ Wash your hands to prevent the spread of germs to yourself or others.

Safety tip:

When caring for a child that appears to be very sick, contact the child's parents for advice, or the doctor if the parents are unavailable. This is especially important when taking care of an infant.

For vomiting:

♦ If a child's stomach feels sick, he or she will usually not feel like eating. Don't give them anything to eat or drink for at least an hour.
♦ A child who begins vomiting will need your assistance. Lay out a towel to protect furniture or get to the toilet.
♦ Help them hold their head over a bowl, towel or the toilet.
♦ When they are not vomiting, encourage them to rest by lying on their side.
♦ Use a cool, wet cloth to wipe the face and lips after vomiting.
♦ Young children and infants who vomit will need to have lost fluids slowly replaced. Get guidelines from the parent or family doctor. *(See safety tip.)*
♦ If a child or infant vomits more than once, contact the parents.
♦ If vomiting is persistent or there's high fever or diarrhea, or you are caring for a sick infant, contact a doctor if you can't contact the parents.
♦ Wash your hands to prevent the spread of germs to yourself or others.

Safety tip:

You might be asked by the parents to replace lost fluids until they get home. Follow their instructions. In general, rest the stomach for one hour, then slowly replace lost fluids with clear liquids. Clear liquids are easier on the stomach in small, frequent amounts such as one tablespoon every 5-10 minutes. Examples include: water, flat soda pop, apple juice, clear broths or soups, jello or Popsicles. Don't give too much, too fast!

Earache

Since children's sinus passages are narrow, they often develop earaches. Symptoms of earaches in children include pain, possible discharge from the ear, fever or hearing loss. Babies may pull at the ear, cry persistently, or refuse to eat.

Action: *Contact parents.*

- Consult with a doctor for diagnosis of an ear infection.
- Report fever and/or ear discharge to parents.
- Comfort an infant by holding and

gently rocking.
- Keep a small child comfortable. Position against pillows, affected ear down.
- For comfort, you may try wrapping a warm water bottle with a towel and apply against the affected ear.
- If you see something lodged in the ear, such as rocks, food or seeds, do not try to remove it. Notify the parents and keep the child comfortable until a medical evaluation can be obtained.

Fever

A fever is when the body becomes unusually hot, often in response to an infection or illness. Symptoms also include chills, irritability, drowsiness and unhappiness. The child may also have a poor appetite, ear pain, rash, diarrhea, or vomiting with a fever. A child may be very ill even if the temperature is not high, so be sure to pay attention to the child's overall health, not just the fever.

Safety tip:

Learn how to use a thermometer and take a temperature. There are two main types of thermometers—digital and mercury. Ask your parents how to use a thermometer. A fever is generally above 100.2 F to 104 F or more.

Action: *Contact parents.*

- Always get advice, especially if you're caring for a sick infant.
- Make sure the child isn't dressed too warmly, and avoid drafts and chills.

- Keep the child comfortable. Be alert to other signs of illness, such as vomiting.
- Replace fluids by giving the child Popsicles, ice chips, clear juices or water. Give small sips and wait at least five minutes to make sure the stomach can handle it.
- If advised, sponge with lukewarm water over the body. Never use cold water as the body can chill and raise the fever.
- You may be advised by the parent to give a non-aspirin product (Acetaminophen), such as Tylenol, to a child in your care to relieve discomfort and reduce fever. Be sure you get clear, written instructions from the parent, including the exact dosage and when to give it. *(See important note on page 57 for information that should be included in instructions.)* This is very important as children do not take the normal adult dosage and there may be other issues such as allergies to medications and stomach problems.
- **Be sure not to give an infant or child, under age 18, any aspirin products.**
- Reassure the ill child and ask the parents to come home if you need them.

Headache

Mild headaches can occur in children in response to changes in temperature, hunger, lack of fluids, fear, rough play, loud noises, injuries or as a sign of illness. Your goal as a sitter is to rest the child in a quiet comfortable area. A cool cloth over the forehead often soothes a mild headache.

A parent should be contacted if pain is unrelieved by rest or the pain is increasing. Urgent medical attention should be obtained if pain is sudden or severe, is the result of a blow to the head, or accompanied with high fever, seizures or unconsciousness.

Action: *Contact the parents if mild. Call 911 if severe.*

♦ Rest the child in a quiet comfortable area.
♦ Apply a cool cloth to the forehead.

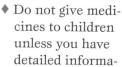

♦ Do not give medicines to children unless you have detailed information from the parents regarding type of medicine, how much, and how often.
♦ **Be sure not to give an infant, or child under age 18, any aspirin products.**
♦ Ask the parents to come home if rest does not relieve headaches, pain is increasing or you suspect illness or injury.
♦ Stay with the child and be supportive until the parent arrives home.

IMPORTANT! If pain is severe, is the result of a blow to the head, or accompanied by high fever, seizures or unconsciousness, seek medical attention immediately (911).

Stomach ache

It is not uncommon for a child to complain of an occasional "tummy ache". Mild stomach pain can be caused by constipation, disagreeable foods, eating and drinking too much or too fast, fear, illness or injury. If a child in your care complains of a stomach ache, stop what you are doing, have the child rest, be supportive and try to get more information.

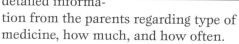

If stomach ache is severe or persistent, with vomiting, fever or bloody stools, the parents should be contacted and medical help obtained.

Action: *Contact the parents. If severe also get medical help.*

♦ Have the child rest in a position of comfort.
♦ Rest the stomach. Do not give anything by mouth.
♦ Have the child use the bathroom if constipated.
♦ For comfort, you may try wrapping a warm water bottle with a towel and apply gently on the abdomen.
♦ If pain is unrelieved by rest or increasing—contact the parents.
♦ Be alert to other signs of illness, such as vomiting or diarrhea—be prepared to help.
♦ If stomach pain is the result of an injury or severe blow to the stomach seek emergency medical support (911).

See important note on page 57 regarding giving medicine to children.

Be prepared—learn first aid and CPR

Although first aid and CPR are covered in later chapters, this book doesn't have space to provide a complete first aid handbook. You should take a class in first aid and CPR. The American Red Cross, American Heart Association and many local hospitals regularly offer classes. You should also take a class on Cardiopulmonary Resuscitation (CPR). In fact, everyone, not just babysitters, should know basic first aid and CPR. Most advanced babysitting classes will teach first aid, CPR and how to handle most childhood emergency health situations.

TIPS FOR SAFETY

In an emergency follow these priorities: Stop. Take a deep breath. Think! If you stay calm the children will feel safer, and you'll be in a better position to make important decisions.

First Aid Guidelines

At some point during your career as a babysitter, you may encounter a child who suffers a mild injury such as a cut or scratch. Your job will be to provide fast, simple first aid to keep the situation from getting worse and lots of calm, tender, loving care. Most youngsters will want you to call their mom or dad just to reassure themselves. Don't hesitate to make the call and write things down so the parents can have all the details.

In the rare situation where a serious illness or injury occurs, you will need to act calmly and quickly to get fast

emergency medical support (911—Fire, Police and Medical Support Number). When in doubt, if simple first aid doesn't help, or the situation is beyond your basic skills, call for help.

In this section we'll cover some basic injuries and the first aid steps to treat them. Again, if you have any doubts about handling an emergency, don't hesitate to call 911 for the emergency medical team in your area.

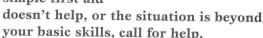

What's a first aid kit?

Every home or work area should have a first aid kit on hand filled with supplies for treating minor injuries. Before you babysit, find out from the parents where the supplies are located. You may also want to store a few special bandages for "boo-boos" in your sitter tote bag.

Take a moment to look through the first aid kit and get instructions for using any unfamiliar first aid product such as cleansing agents, chemicals or thermometers. Let the parents know when you've used the first aid kit so they can replenish supplies as needed.

Ask the parents for a set of emergency phone numbers, and get brief medical information for each child, including allergies. Gather any other information that may be helpful to a trained healthcare provider in case an accident occurs.

Supplies often found in first aid kits:

- ✗ Adhesive tape
- ✗ Antiseptic cream
- ✗ Bandages—various sizes
- ✗ Bandages—soft gauze pads
- ✗ Cleansing agents, such as mild soap
- ✗ Eye pads, eye wash
- ✗ First aid book
- ✗ Gloves—disposable
- ✗ Ipecac syrup/activated charcoal
- ✗ Roller gauze
- ✗ Scissors
- ✗ Splinter tweezers
- ✗ Safety pins—all sizes
- ✗ Tape—waterproof and various sizes
- ✗ Thermometer
- ✗ Tongue blades

Allergic reactions

An allergic reaction can occur from anything a child inhaled, swallowed or applied to the skin. You should ask the parents about any known allergies and avoid these items. A child who develops a mild allergy may exhibit itching, rash or sneezing. If the allergic reaction is severe, a child may experience trouble swallowing, shortness of breath, weakness, hives, facial swelling or unconsciousness. Common causes of allergy in children include nuts, pollen, bee stings or medications.

Action:

❖ If there is an itchy rash, discourage scratching. Apply a cold pack *(see below)* to the area to help decrease itching and swelling.
❖ Do not give or apply medicines unless you receive clear instructions from the parents.
❖ Call parents if mild or call 911 if symptoms are severe, especially facial swelling, shortness of breath, confusion or weakness.

Bee stings and bug bites

During the summer months the most common offenders of bites and stings are bees, yellow jackets, mosquitoes, spiders and flies. A child may complain of a raised bite or sting area with pain, itching, rash, swelling or redness. Bee stings and bug bites are usually not dangerous but can be irritating and painful.

Severe bee sting reactions can be life threatening to children who are allergic to them. If the child is allergic he or she may experience difficulty breathing or swallowing, hives, excessive swelling or itching at the site, facial swelling, pale or bluish skin, dizziness or weakness. **If a child has a known bee allergy, don't wait for symptoms to occur, call 911 immediately.**

Action: *Contact parent if symptoms are minor. If allergic call 911 immediately!*

❖ Calm the child.
❖ Scrape off the stinger (if bee sting) as soon as possible with a fingernail, but don't squeeze or pinch it.
❖ Wash the site with mild soap and water.
❖ Apply a cold pack or cool cloth to reduce pain, itching and swelling. (See *tip below*.)
❖ Contact the parents if symptoms are minor and let them know how things are going. Continue to reassure the child.
❖ If the child receives multiple stings (especially around the face and neck), or the child has a known bee allergy or begins to show signs of a severe reaction, don't wait for symptoms to occur, call 911 immediately for advice!

Tip: How to make a cold pack

Icing the area with a cold compress can reduce pain and swelling if used properly. To make a cold pack, use a wash cloth rinsed in cold water or fill a small baggie with some ice chips and use as an ice bag. Use a barrier, like a dishtowel, to wrap around the ice bag to keep the skin from getting too cold. Ice for no longer than 10-20 minutes at a time and check the skin frequently to avoid further injury.

Bites (animal/human)

Teach children to be careful around unfamiliar animals. If a child gets bitten, look for a break in the skin. There may be a small puncture wound or a deep, bleeding, painful wound. In either case, you will want to stop the bleeding, then clean the wound to prevent infection. Contact a parent when a bite breaks the skin.

Action: *Contact parents for minor injury, call 911 for serious injury.*

❖ Calm the child.
❖ Stop bleeding by applying direct pressure over the break in the skin with a clean cloth like a dishtowel, about 5-10 minutes.

❖ When bleeding has stopped. Wash with mild soap and cool (not icy or hot) water.
❖ Call for advice from the parent or 911, especially if a bite breaks the skin.
❖ Always report bites to the parents whether or not it has broken the skin.
❖ If necessary, contact animal control for help in handling the offending animal.

Safety tip:
Never leave small children unattended around animals—even the family pet. Do not befriend wild animals such as squirrels, raccoons or skunks.

Burns

Minor burns are often treated safely at home and affect only the top layer of skin. The burn site can be painful, warm to touch, pink or reddened without blisters, and may swell. A sunburn is an example of a minor burn. Serious burns can cause discoloration, blistering or charring of the skin. These burns go below the top layers of skin and can be quite painful. **Serious burns can't be treated safely at home and require immediate medical attention.**

Action: *Call parents or 911.*

❖ Gently flush in cool—not icy—water. Rinse until the burn edges are cool to touch or pain subsides (about 15-20 minutes or more).
❖ Don't apply butter or creams to the burn. Gently remove clothing off the burn site only if clothing is not stuck to wound.
❖ If after cooling there are open blisters or charred skin, lightly cover burn with dry clean bandage. *Get help by calling 911 as soon as possible.*

Call parents if:
❖ The burn causes a blister.
❖ The burn is on the face, legs, hand, feet or groin.
❖ The burn is larger than the child's open hand.

Call 911 if:
❖ The burn covers a large portion of the body.
❖ There is charred skin or large, open blisters.
❖ The child is weak.
❖ Clothing is stuck to the skin.
❖ You can't locate the parents.

Safety tip:

Watch for items that could burn a child, such as pots on the stove, steam or matches, and remove them from reach. Don't carry hot liquids around small children or infants.

First Aid Guidelines

Chest pain

Chest pain most often occurs in adults, but is something you should definitely be aware of when babysitting. Symptoms can include a complaint of tightness, pressure, or squeezing chest pain lasting up to two minutes that can radiate to either arm or lower jaw. There may be difficulty breathing and/or sweating, nausea or weakness.

Action: *Contact 911. Get emergency help fast!*

❖ Stop activity and have the person sit down and rest.
❖ Call 911 immediately especially if chest pain is constant and not relieved by 1-2 minutes or rest.
❖ Stay on the phone with 911 and follow their instructions.
❖ If not breathing, begin mouth-to-mouth breathing.
❖ If there's no pulse, begin CPR if trained.

Choking

See section: "Suffocation and Choking," page 75.

Safety tip:
To avoid choking situations, discourage young children from eating and running around at the same time. Survey each room for any choking hazards, such as nuts, coins, pins, small toys, balloons and paper clips, and take the time to put all items out of reach.

Convulsions (seizures)

A seizure may be caused by a temporary irritant to the brain such as a high fever, viral infection, head injury, drug reaction or by epilepsy. **Most seizures don't last more than five minutes in children.** Symptoms can include loss of consciousness, eyes that blink, stare or roll back, twitching, jerky movements, muscle stiffness, loss of bladder or bowel control and temporary breath holding. Convulsions can look alarming, so you should always calmly call for medical advice.

Action: *Contact 911 for emergency medical support, then the parents.*

❖ Stay as calm as possible. Reassure the child. Call for help.
❖ Move clutter and/or furniture to protect the child from injury.
❖ Loosen tight fitting clothing especially around the neck.
❖ Don't put anything in their mouth, especially your fingers.
❖ Gently roll the child onto the side to allow saliva to flow out of the mouth.
❖ Try to note what happened during the seizure and how long it lasted.
❖ As the convulsion stops, be available to comfort the youngster who may be confused for a while after a seizure.
❖ After obtaining medical advice, notify the parents as soon as possible.

Cuts and bruises (minor)

If a child is bleeding, you need to stop the flow of blood by applying direct pressure over the cut. You will also need to clean the cut so it will not become infected and put on a bandage to prevent further injury. **Don't be alarmed by the site of blood, since the child needs your calm support.**

Action: If bleeding or swelling is severe or located in sensitive areas such as the face, neck or groin, cuts are ¹/₂ inch wide or deeper, or cuts are dirty and difficult to clean—call 911 and the parents right away!

Mild cuts or abrasions: Stop bleeding by applying direct pressure over the break in the skin with a clean cloth like a clean dish-towel for 5-10 minutes. After bleeding has stopped, gently clean with mild soap and cool (not icy or hot) water. Cover the clean wound with a sterile bandage, like a Band-aid.

Bruises: Rest the injury. Prepare a cold pack *(see page 64)* and apply gently over the affected area to decrease pain and swelling. Elevate injured area if it does not cause pain.

Drowning

Infants and children can drown in just a few inches of water. The best single protection against drowning is constant babysitter and adult supervision. You can't rely on life jackets and floats to keep a child safe. If you can't swim, don't have CPR training or have too many kids to watch, the safest thing to do is to tell the parents you don't feel qualified to watch kids around water.

What if you find a child in your care face down in water? Get the child out of the water immediately, but do it safely. Don't put yourself at risk if you don't swim. Check whether or not the child is breathing or has a heartbeat. Call for help (911). If you know how, immediately begin CPR if there is no breathing or heartbeat.

What if you pull a child out of the water and he or she seems to recover? A child who has nearly drowned and appears okay should still be checked out. A child found face down in water may have swallowed water into the stomach and lungs. The fluid in the lungs can lead to later complications such as pneumonia or lung collapse.

Action: *Call 911 immediately!*

❖ Act quickly to safely remove the child from the water.
❖ If not breathing, begin mouth-to-mouth breathing. Call for help. If no pulse, begin CPR if trained.
❖ Once revived, keep the child warm. As children recover they may spit up water or vomit. Gently roll the child to the side to clear the mouth and maintain clear breathing passages.
❖ In cases of near-drowning, always get medical assistance, even if the child looks fine, to avoid delayed problems.
❖ Stay with the child until help arrives. Contact the parents as soon as possible.

Safety tip:
An infant or child can drown in just a few inches of water. Never leave an infant or child alone around any water source, including puddles, buckets, bathtubs, toilets, swimming pools or hot tubs, not even for a second.

First Aid Guidelines

Electric shock

Electrical shocks can occur if someone comes in direct contact with an electric current. If a child is shocked, you may see burns at the point of contact. These kinds of burns can be very serious. Other signs of a more severe electric shock may be pain, unconsciousness and breathing difficulty. You might see muscle spasms or seizure activity. **Getting help is top priority.** If the child is alert without sign of burn or injury, contact the parents to let them know.

Action: *Contact parents if child has no sign of injury, 911 if severe.*

- ❖ Think! Don't touch the child if there's still contact with the source of electricity.
- ❖ Break contact with electrical source quickly using dry wood or a non-metal object. Call for help!

- ❖ If the child is not seriously injured, be supportive and call the parents.
- ❖ Check the child over—if you see any burns apply simple first aid and call for medical support.
- ❖ If the child is not breathing, call 911 for help immediately. Begin mouth-to-mouth breathing if you know how. If no pulse, begin CPR if trained.

Safety tip:
To avoid electric shock, cover unused electrical outlets, move or unplug frayed cords, remove electrical appliances out of reach, and eliminate other hazards.

Eye injury

An eye injury can result from a particle, such as sand or dirt, blowing into the eye, by a sharp object puncturing the eye, or a liquid or chemical splashing into the eye. Symptoms can include a watery, irritated, or painful eye, reluctance to open the eye, or a foreign object that is visible or protruding from the eye. *Cleaning solutions or other burning chemicals can cause serious injury to the eye so it's imperative that you act quickly.*

Action: *Contact parents if eye injury is simple and pain persists. Contact 911 if the eye injury is severe or involves a chemical.*

- ❖ Begin with a hug for comfort and to prevent the child from rubbing the injured eye.
- ❖ To treat a simple eye injury, put a cool cloth or small cold pack on the eye and contact the parents for advice.

- ❖ A child's tears will often wash out small particles from the eye. You can also gently flush the eye out by pouring clean lukewarm water from a cup into the eye to clean it out.
If pain persists, get medical help.
- ❖ If a liquid such as a chemical splashes into the eye, it may begin to burn. Act fast. Lay the child on his or her back. Begin gentle flushing of the eyeball with small cups of water for up to 15-20 minutes. Pour from the inside corner of the eye toward the outside, away from the unaffected eye. Call 911 for help.
- ❖ If you can see an object is stuck in the eye, don't try to remove it. Protect the eye from further injury by keeping the child's hands away from the eye. Call 911 for help.

Fainting

Fainting is a temporary loss of consciousness caused by a momentary lack of blood supply to the brain, often with a pooling of blood in the legs. Fainting spells can take us by surprise but are usually short in duration and not life threatening. Some causes can be panic, fear, over-breathing, heat exhaustion, hunger, pain or even illness.

Action: *Contact parents. Contact 911, especially if the child does not wake up fast, or is confused for more than a few minutes.*

❖ Gently lay the child flat, elevate legs above the level of the heart.
❖ Watch breathing, check pulse. Child should regain consciousness within 30 seconds.
❖ Have the child take slow, deep breaths. Loosen clothing for comfort.
❖ Once alert, sit the child up slowly for several minutes and reassure him or her.
❖ Try to recall the cause for fainting and write down how long the spell lasted.
❖ Notify the parents about the fainting spell.
❖ **If the child does not wake up fast, or is confused for more than a few minutes, call for help (911). Get advice!**

Fractures and sprains

It is often difficult to know if an injury is a fracture, sprain or strain. Signs to look for include severe pain, swelling, redness or bruising. A child who has a fracture may or may not have an open cut, misshapen area or inability to use the injured area. **To be safe, apply first aid to keep things from getting worse until the injury can be checked out.**

Action: *Contact 911 and parents.*
❖ Calm the child. Have the child rest in a position of comfort.
❖ Check location and inspect for pain, swelling, unusual position or bruising.
❖ Keep the injured area from moving if you think it might be broken or sprained.
❖ Apply a cold pack to site *(see page 64)* to help to decrease pain and swelling.
❖ Call for advice.

Head injury

It is not easy to tell if a head injury is serious. Many times children fall, bump their heads, cry for a few minutes, then go back playing. **Your job is to make note of all head injuries and tell the parents about them.** If a head injury is serious you will often note a change in their behavior. Serious symptoms can include unconsciousness or confusion, vomiting, severe headache, pallor, sleepiness, uneven pupils or breathing difficulties. If the blow was severe, call for help even if the child seems fine. **Always report even minor injuries to parents.**

Action: *Call 911 and the parents.*
❖ Have the child rest for several minutes and note their behavior. Look for bumps, cuts or bruises. Stop any bleeding you see.
❖ To treat a bump on the head, wrap some ice in a clean cloth and rest it on the bump. Contact the parents.
❖ Treat any serious head injury as an emergency. Call 911 for help. Stay with the child and keep them comfortable.
❖ Monitor closely for unconsciousness.
❖ Watch for changing behavior: drowsiness, excessive crying, irritability or confusion.

First Aid Guidelines

Hypothermia (cold exposure)

Children loose heat faster than adults do, and young children can't often tell you when they feel cold. Therefore, it's up to you to anticipate bad weather days and act to prevent cold exposure from occurring. Symptoms of hypothermia can include persistent shivering, irritability, discomfort, slow or slurred speech, memory lapses, frequent stumbling, confusion, drowsiness, and exhaustion.

Action: *Call parents if mild, 911 if cold exposure was prolonged and symptoms worsen.*

❖ Get the child out of the cold. Seek shelter.
❖ Change to warm, dry clothing. Apply warm blankets and cover the head with a warm cap. Body to body heat may also be helpful.
❖ If alert, encourage the child to drink fluids such as warm soups and juices.
❖ Try to keep the child calm and avoid exertion.
❖ Always contact a doctor if cold exposure was prolonged and symptoms worsen.

Nosebleed

An injury, illness, sneezing, picking or excessive blowing of the nose can lead to a bloody nose. *A nosebleed is not usually serious, but can be frightening to a child.*

Action: *Contact parents or 911 for advice.*
❖ Calm the child.

❖ Try to get the child comfortable standing or sitting with head slightly forward.
❖ Squeeze the nose closed for 5-10 minutes. Use a barrier like a tissue to protect your hands from the blood.
❖ If bleeding does not stop after 10 minutes, reapply pressure and call for advice.
❖ Discourage young children from blowing or picking their nose after a bleed.

Poisoning

If you suspect an accidental poisoning, don't wait for symptoms to occur. Signs to be aware of include vomiting or diarrhea, irritability, sweating, convulsions, pain, nausea, confusion or unconsciousness.

Action: *Don't wait for symptoms to occur—contact 911 or local poison control for advice at once, then call the parents!*
❖ When calling, state this is an emergency and be prepared to give your location.
❖ Take the child and whatever they ate or drank to the phone with you. Take the bottle or container even if it is empty.

❖ Follow instructions. Stay on the line and report the status of the child.
❖ Reassure the child; notify the parents.

Safety tip:
If you think something might be a hazard, be on the safe side and put it out of children's reach. Some household poisons include alcohol, ammonia, bug spray, cleaners, perfume, soaps, fingernail polish, moth balls, certain plants, vitamins and other medicines.

Sunburn

Prevention is the key to avoiding sunburn. Keep small children out of direct sun contact during peak sun hours (between 10:00 a.m. and 2:00 p.m.) and use cover-ups such as hats, umbrellas, and light protective clothing when going outside. Signs of sunburn are red, painful and warm skin. If the burn is severe, blisters will form, and the child may have chills.

Action: *Contact parents for advice.*
❖ Apply cool compresses or bathe in cool (not icy) water. Call for advice.

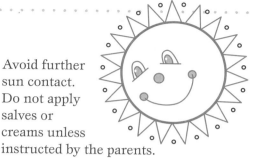

❖ Avoid further sun contact. Do not apply salves or creams unless instructed by the parents.
❖ Encourage the child to drink fluids.
❖ Contact the parents especially if the burn covers a large area of the body or there are blisters.
❖ If severe: contact 911.

Safety tip:
Apply an approved sunscreen provided by the parents at least a half-hour before going outdoors so it has time to absorb into the skin. Do not apply sunscreen to infants less than six months. Make sure the kids drink plenty of fluids when they're out in the sun.

Toothache

Symptoms of a toothache may include sensitivity to heat, cold and sweets. There may also be pain or facial swelling.

Action: *Contact parents.*
❖ Apply a cold pack to the face over the affected area.
❖ Get advice when there is fever, pain or continued sensitivities.
❖ Avoid foods or fluids that cause discomfort.
❖ Let the parents know about the toothache as soon as possible.

Safety tip:
For quick reference keep emergency numbers handy, near the phone or in your pocket.

In an emergency stop, breath and think! Stay calm.

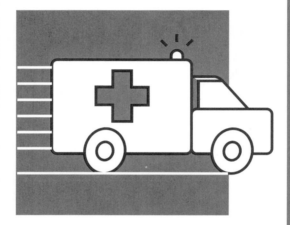

TIPS FOR SAFETY ---> First aid can help keep injuries from becoming serious and make the child more comfortable until you can get help. Always add TLC— Tender, Loving Care!

Emergency Guidelines

In an emergency, follow these priorities:

Stop! Take a deep breath and think!

1 Look at each emergency situation individually. Is there danger? Could there be a head, neck or spinal injury? Don't move the victim unless necessary, since movement could cause more injury. Respond to life-threatening injuries first.

2 Check for a response. Ask the child, "Are you okay?" If you need help, yell loudly for assistance or use a nearby telephone to call 911.

3 Check the airway for breathing. If the child is not breathing, begin mouth-to-mouth breathing immediately, if you know how.

4 Check the pulse. If none, begin CPR if you know how.

5 Check for bleeding. Stop bleeding by applying direct pressure over the wound, using a barrier such as a clean cloth or absorbent bandage. Wear gloves if available.

6 Check for health problems. Look for medical ID tags that describe allergies or special conditions such as diabetes or seizure disorder.

7 Do not give fluids. If the victim is unconscious he/she will not be able to swallow and could choke.

8 Use simple techniques, such as keeping the victim warm, until professional medical help arrives.

9 Stay calm and don't give up. Continue to aid the victim until help arrives!

REMEMBER! Your actions save lives!

When you care for small children, always watch out for items they could put in their mouths and put those items out of reach.

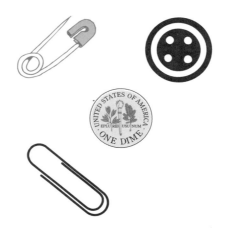

TIPS FOR SAFETY

You should know what to do if a child stops breathing... Take a class in **CPR** and learn the **ABCs**— Airway, Breathing and Circulation.

Suffocation and Choking

Choking and suffocation are two of the most common accidents that can happen to infants and children today. Most of these accidents can be prevented by recognizing potential hazards and taking steps to reduce them.

Suffocation

Suffocation is the lack of oxygen to the brain that can occur when someone is strangled, chokes, or becomes trapped in a small space without enough oxygen.

Action:

✦ Finding a child who has suffocated can be scary, so stop, take a deep breath and think!

✦ First remove any items causing the child to suffocate.

✦ Check for a response. Ask, "Are you okay?"

✦ If no response, get help immediately! Yell for help if necessary!

✦ Call 911 (emergency medical support) as soon as possible.

✦ Check the ABCs: Airway, Breathing and Circulation (pulse).

✦ If there's no pulse or breathing, begin CPR immediately and continue uninterrupted until help arrives.

✦ If you don't know what to do, don't delay in calling 911 and stay on the line. The medical team will tell you what to do.

✦ If you haven't learned CPR (cardiopulmonary resuscitation), take a CPR class to learn and practice the skills on a training mannequin.

Look for these common hazards and remove whenever possible:

➤ Drapery cords and extension cords.

➤ Plastic bags, such as those from the grocery store or cleaners.

➤ Toys or jewelry that hang around a child's neck.

➤ Toys or pacifiers with a string longer than 12 inches.

➤ Crib gyms. These should be removed from cribs once an infant is able to pull up on his or her hands and knees.

➤ Old appliances, such as refrigerators, where a child could become trapped and suffocate. Look out for anything that can't be opened from the inside.

Choking

Choking occurs when an infant or child inhales food or a small object, blocking the airway and making it difficult or impossible to breathe. Young infants and children tend to put more things in their mouths as they learn about the world they live in and seem to have the most trouble with items that are smooth, slippery, hard, round or just the right size to plug their throat. Basically, kids can choke on just about anything small!

Some common items an infant or child can choke on include:

Balloons, beads, buttons, coins, hard candies, hot dogs, marbles, paper clips, peanuts, plastic wrappers, popcorn, raisins, raw vegetables, sticky substances such as marshmallows or gummy bears, tacks or small toys. What else can you think of?

_____

_____

_____

Prevention:

When you care for small children, always be on the lookout for items they could put into their mouths. Put away items children could choke on and keep an eye on them when they eat. Check toys for loose parts and put them away if they need repair. At mealtime, try to encourage the children to sit at the table, avoid rough play, and cut food into small pieces for easy chewing and swallowing. Stay with the children while they eat so if they choke you can assist them. Also, don't let them run around with anything in their mouths, as they could fall and get items lodged in their throats.

You should know what to do if an infant or child chokes or is not breathing.

*In the next few pages, we'll review guidelines for treatment of choking and CPR (cardiopulmonary resuscitation) for those already trained in CPR. **This information will not teach you how to do CPR. You really need to take a course to get hands-on CPR practice.** If you haven't taken a course, this information will familiarize you with the techniques necessary to save a life and prepare you for this most valuable class. Classes on CPR are available through health agencies, schools and fire departments. Generally, these courses also cover how to clear a victim's breathing passages and rescue breathing techniques.*

Don't ever practice CPR skills on the children you are babysitting. Practice should only occur in the classroom using training mannequins!

Taking care of a choking child

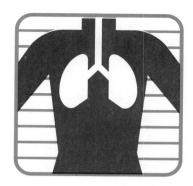

It's normal for an infant or child to cough if something is in the airway, so first check to see if the victim needs help. If the child doesn't need help and is just coughing normally, attempting to help clear the child's airway can actually do more harm than good.

To find out whether the child needs help, do an assessment:

✦ Ask if the child can speak, cough or breathe. If the child is coughing forcefully, don't interfere. Continue to watch the child carefully.

✦ Monitor for signs of an obstructed airway. This can be quiet wheezing, gagging, a weak cough, or no sound at all as the object stuck in the throat makes the child unable to speak or breathe. The child may panic and may also begin changing colors. The face may start to look blue, especially around the mouth.

✦ If the child can't breathe, cough, or speak, clear a victim's breathing passage by performing a rescue breathing technique—only if you know how or have been trained! If you don't know what to do, call 911.

✦ Call 911 or local emergency number IMMEDIATELY if the child still can't cough forcefully, speak or breathe. Keep trying to perform a rescue breathing technique while waiting for help to arrive.

Remember: Don't put your finger down the child's throat if you can't see what's there. You may push an item further back into the airway, making it even harder to remove.

Performing a rescue breathing technique

Even if the victim has just exhaled, there's still a considerable supply of air in the lungs beneath the obstruction. When you clear a victim's breathing passages you make use of the leftover air in the lungs to create an artificial cough, forcing the object up through the throat and out of the mouth.

➤ You should know what to do if an infant or child chokes or is not breathing. Be prepared—take a course in CPR.

How do I tell
if a child is choking?

A child who is choking will not be able to effectively cough, speak or breathe. There can be quiet wheezing, gagging, a weak cough, or no sound at all as the object stuck in the throat makes the child unable to speak or breathe. The child may panic and may also begin changing colors. The face may start to look blue, especially around the mouth.

When do you use a rescue
breathing technique on a child
who is choking?

If a child appears to be choking and is coughing forcefully, don't interfere with the child's efforts to clear his or her airway. You should stay nearby and be ready to help with a rescue breathing technique when the cough becomes weak, or the child is unable to speak or breathe. **If you don't know how to perform a rescue breathing technique, call 911 and follow instructions.** Take a class in CPR so you will know what to do.

Don't put your finger down the child's throat if you can't see what's there. You may push the item further back into the airway, making it even harder to remove.

Choking; conscious baby—birth to one year

The rescue breathing technique for a choking infant is a series of five blows to the back and five thrusts to the chest.

First, determine whether or not the infant is able to cough, cry or breathe. If the baby can't breathe or cry, or is turning a bluish color, act quickly!

1 Lay the baby face down with the head lower than the chest. Support the head with your hand around the jaw and under the chest. Rest your arm on your thigh. Give five back blows with the heel of your hand between the shoulder blades. This means hitting the baby firmly but not hard enough to hurt.

2 If these blows don't work and the object is still stuck, carefully turn the infant over onto your other arm by supporting the infant's head, neck, and jaw with one hand, and the back, neck, and head with the other hand. The baby should be securely sandwiched and supported between your arms as you carefully turn him or her over onto the back, face up. Position the baby on your arm resting on your thigh, with the head lower than the chest.

3 Deliver five chest thrusts with two or three fingertips, positioning the fingers on the center of the baby's chest, one finger width below the baby's nipples. Push the breastbone in the center of the baby's chest down 1/2 inch to 1 inch to create an artificial cough. This may force the object out of the baby's windpipe.

4 Keep repeating five back blows and five chest thrusts until the object comes out or the baby becomes unconscious. Be persistent! **Notify 911 immediately even if the baby recovers.**

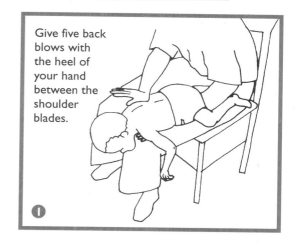

Give five back blows with the heel of your hand between the shoulder blades.

1

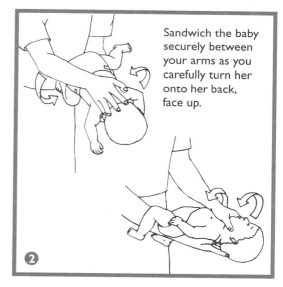

Sandwich the baby securely between your arms as you carefully turn her onto her back, face up.

2

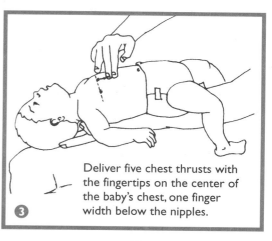

Deliver five chest thrusts with the fingertips on the center of the baby's chest, one finger width below the nipples.

3

Suffocation and Choking

Choking; conscious child—one year to adult

The rescue breathing technique for children over one year and adults is called the Heimlich maneuver. The Heimlich maneuver is a series of inward and upward thrusts performed below the rib cage and above the navel (mid-abdomen) to dislodge the object.

First ask the victim, "Are you okay?" If the victim is coughing hard and can speak, stay nearby but don't perform the maneuver.

Look for signs of choking such as a weak cough, bluish lips, and inability to speak. When the victim isn't able to cough, speak, or breathe and/or is turning blue in the face, lips, mouth, or nose, quickly perform the Heimlich maneuver, instructions below.

The Heimlich maneuver

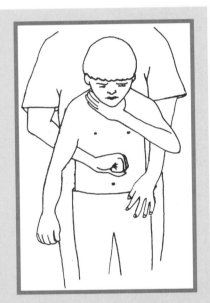

1 Stand or kneel behind the child.

2 Make a fist with one hand and place the thumb side of the fist below the rib cage and above the belly button.

3 Cover the fist with your other hand and thrust inward and upward.

4 Don't push on the rib cage.

5 Begin with 5-10 inward and upward thrusts.

6 Repeat the thrusts until the object comes out and the child recovers, or until the child becomes unconscious or limp in your arms.

7 Be persistent!

8 If the child becomes unconscious gently lay him or her down and go directly to the phone and call 911 for emergency help!

9 Check the ABCs—Airway, Breathing, Circulation (pulse). You'll need to determine if the airway is still blocked by performing a careful assessment.

10 Be sure to follow the emergency operator's instructions.

11 Let a doctor and the parent know right away what happened and how the child was treated—even if he or she recovers and looks fine.

Note: *The above maneuvers should never be practiced on non-choking victims. They should be practiced only on training mannequins in an approved airway management maneuvers class.*

Maybe the child you're taking care of looks like he or she is choking. If you're not sure, here are a few questions to help you decide what to do.

How do I tell if a child is choking?

A child who is choking will not be able to effectively cough, speak or breathe. There can be quiet wheezing, gagging, a weak cough, or no sound at all as the object stuck in the throat makes the child unable to speak or breathe. The child may panic and may also begin changing colors. The face may start to look blue, especially around the mouth.

What if the child has a fever, has been ill, and has a barky cough, drooling secretions, and wheezing respirations?

Call 911 the emergency medical support team immediately!

What if a child is coughing forcefully? Should I interfere?

If a child appears to be choking and is coughing forcefully, don't interfere with the child's efforts to clear his or her airway. You should stay nearby and be ready to help with a rescue breathing technique when the cough becomes weak, or the child is unable to speak or breathe. If you don't know how to perform a rescue breathing technique, call 911 and follow instructions. Take a class in CPR so you will know what to do.

What if the child can't speak or cry, isn't coughing very well, and makes a high-pitched sound when trying to breathe?

When the cough becomes weak, or the child is unable to speak or breathe, begin the rescue breathing technique described on pages 79-80 that is appropriate for their age, if you have had training. Call 911 as soon as possible, especially if you don't know what to do.

TIPS FOR SAFETY ----▶ If you don't know what to do, call 911 immediately!

Suffocation and Choking

CPR is one of the most important life-saving techniques you should know.

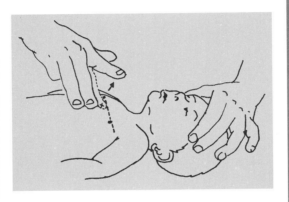

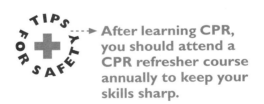

TIPS FOR SAFETY

→ After learning CPR, you should attend a CPR refresher course annually to keep your skills sharp.

CPR-Cardiopulmonary Resuscitation

As a babysitter, you especially need to take the time to complete a CPR course. An accident or sudden illness can happen at any time, and you should be prepared to handle emergencies. You're responsible for taking care of other people's children—while the parents are away the children are completely dependent on your care.

The following are some CPR guidelines for infants and children. **These guidelines shouldn't replace a CPR program, but should be used to refresh your memory.** CPR classes teach you how to help someone who is not breathing and who does not have a measurable pulse. Classes are available from your local fire department, school or health agency. After learning CPR, you should attend a CPR refresher class every year to keep your skills up-to-date.

Matthew Brine has successfully completed the CPR — Cardiopulmonary Resuscitation Course

CPR Class

Infant CPR—less than one year

To begin, check for response. If the infant isn't breathing and doesn't have a pulse, call 911 and begin CPR. Perform CPR on a firm, flat surface.

Basic CPR guidelines

1 If the infant is unconscious, **open the airway** by gently tilting the head and lifting the chin.

2 **Check for breathing.** Look, listen and feel for breathing. If the infant isn't breathing, make a seal with your mouth over the baby's mouth and nose. *Give the baby two breaths to see if the chest rises.* If the chest doesn't rise after the first two breaths, reposition the head (making sure the airway is open) and try again. If the chest still doesn't rise, the airway may be blocked and you'll need to perform a rescue breathing technique if you know how *(see page 77)*.

3 **Check the infant's arm for a brachial pulse, with two fingers and not your thumb.** If you use your thumb you could pick up your own pulse. *Note: The pulse is the rhythmical throbbing of arteries produced by the regular contractions of the heart, and is felt in the neck, wrist or baby's arm. The pulse tells us the heart is beating.*

4 **If there is a pulse but the infant isn't breathing, begin rescue breathing—** one breath every three seconds. (Rate of 20 per minute).

5 **If there's no pulse, begin CPR if trained.** If you haven't been trained or don't know what to do, call 911 immediately for instructions.

✦ Compress the breast bone (sternum) $1/2$ inch to 1 inch, using two or three fingers just below the nipple line.

✦ Perform five chest compressions to every breath for one minute. (Rate of 100 compressions to 20 breaths per minute). If you haven't already called for help, CALL 911 NOW!

✦ Re-check the pulse after the first minute of CPR and continue CPR if needed until help arrives.

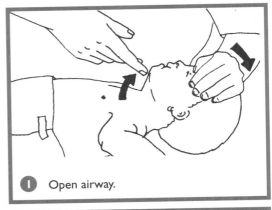

1 Open airway.

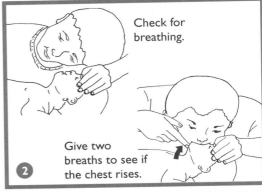

Check for breathing.

Give two breaths to see if **2** the chest rises.

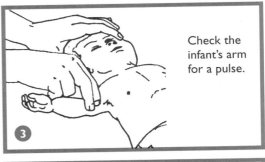

Check the infant's arm for a pulse.

3

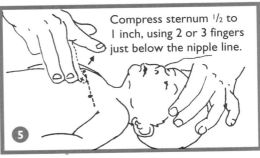

Compress sternum $1/2$ to 1 inch, using 2 or 3 fingers just below the nipple line.

5

CPR—Cardiopulmonary Resuscitation

Child CPR—one to eight years

To begin, check for response. If the child isn't breathing and doesn't have a pulse, call 911 and begin CPR. Perform CPR on a firm, flat surface.

Basic CPR guidelines

1 If the child is unconscious, **open the airway** by gently tilting the head and lifting the chin.

2 **Check for breathing.** Look, listen and feel for breathing. If the child is not breathing, make a seal with your mouth over the child's mouth and pinch the nostrils closed. *Give the child two slow breaths to see if the chest rises.* If the chest does not rise after the first two breaths, reposition the head (making sure the airway is open) and try again. If the chest still doesn't rise, the airway may be blocked and you'll need to perform a rescue breathing technique—only if you know how *(see page 77).*

3 **Check the neck for a carotid pulse, with two fingers and not your thumb.** If you use your thumb you may pick up your own pulse. *Note: The pulse is the rhythmical throbbing of arteries produced by regular contractions of the heart, and is felt in the neck, wrist or arm. The pulse tells us the heart is beating.*

4 **If there is a pulse but the child is not breathing, begin rescue breathing—**one breath every three seconds. (Rate of 20 per minute.)

5 **If there is no pulse begin CPR right away**—only if you're trained. If you haven't been trained or don't know what to do, call 911 immediately for instructions.

✦ Carefully locate landmarks for chest compressions. Run finger up the lower rib margin of the rib cage and locate the sternal notch where both sides of the ribs come together. Place the heel of your hand above the notch on the sternum or center of the chest.

✦ Compress mid-sternum 1-1$\frac{1}{2}$ inches, using the heel of one hand, vertically downward.

✦ Perform five chest compressions to every breath for one minute. (Rate of 100 compressions to 20 breaths per minute). **If you haven't already called for help, call 911 immediately!**

✦ Re-check the pulse after one minute of CPR and continue CPR (if needed) until help arrives.

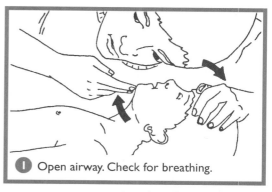

1 Open airway. Check for breathing.

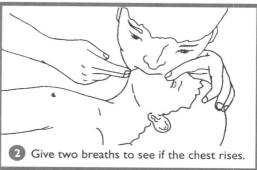

2 Give two breaths to see if the chest rises.

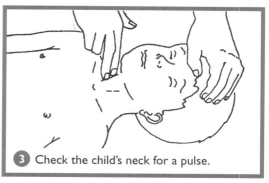

3 Check the child's neck for a pulse.

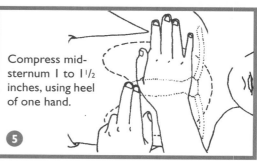

Compress mid-sternum 1 to 1$\frac{1}{2}$ inches, using heel of one hand.

5

CPR—Cardiopulmonary Resuscitation

Adult CPR—older child, adolescent, adult

To begin, check for a response. If the victim isn't breathing and doesn't have a pulse, call 911 and begin CPR. Perform CPR on a firm, flat surface.

Basic CPR guidelines

① If the victim is unconscious, **open the airway** by gently tilting the head and lifting the chin.

② **Check for breathing.** Look, listen and feel for breathing. If the child or adult is not breathing, make a seal with your mouth over the mouth and pinch the nostrils closed. *Give the victim two slow breaths to see if the chest rises.* If the chest does not rise after the first two breaths, reposition the head (make sure the airway is open) and try again. If the chest still doesn't rise, the airway may be blocked and you'll need to perform a rescue breathing technique if you know how *(see page 77).*

③ **Check the neck for a carotid pulse, with two fingers and not your thumb.** If you use your thumb you could pick up your own pulse. *Note: The pulse is the rhythmical throbbing of arteries produced by the regular contractions of the heart, and is felt in the neck, wrist or arm. The pulse tells us the heart is beating.*

④ **If there is a pulse but the victim is not breathing, begin rescue breathing—** one breath every five seconds. (Rate of 12 breaths per minute.)

⑤ **If there is no pulse, call 911 now and begin CPR right away.**

◆ Carefully locate landmarks for chest compressions. Run fingers up the lower rib margin of the rib cage and locate the sternal notch where both sides of the ribs come together. Place the heel of your hand above the notch on the sternum or center of the chest. Place your second hand on top of the first.

◆ Compress mid-sternum 1½-2 inches, using two hands vertically downward.

◆ Perform 15 chest compressions to every two full breaths for one minute. (Rate of 80-100 compressions to 12 breaths per minute).

◆ Re-check the pulse and continue CPR (if needed) until help arrives.

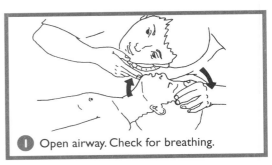

① Open airway. Check for breathing.

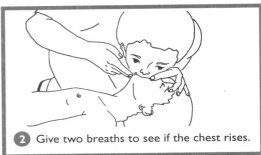

② Give two breaths to see if the chest rises.

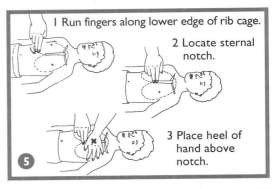

1 Run fingers along lower edge of rib cage.

2 Locate sternal notch.

3 Place heel of hand above notch.

⑤

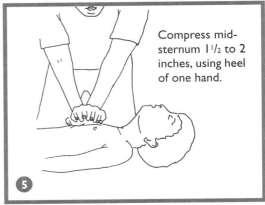

Compress mid-sternum 1½ to 2 inches, using heel of one hand.

⑤

CPR—Cardiopulmonary Resuscitation

CPR questions and answers

How does CPR work?
CPR helps keep victims breathing and their heart beating after they become unconscious and these functions have stopped. CPR keeps them alive until medical help is available. In CPR, the breaths you give provide oxygen to the body and the compressions cause artificial circulation to take place, carrying the oxygen to vital organs.

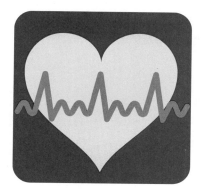

How can I be sure a child needs to receive CPR?
Children need CPR if they're unconscious, not breathing, and don't have a pulse. If they're not breathing but have a heartbeat, they will not need full CPR (both chest compressions and artificial breaths) but may need rescue breathing. You need to know how to check the signs to be able to assess whether CPR is needed or not.

Should I start CPR right away if I find a child unconscious?
No—children may become unconscious for a number of reasons. Always check to see if they're not breathing (look, listen and feel for breathing) and don't have a pulse before performing CPR.

What is rescue breathing?
Rescue breathing is performed after the determining the victim has a pulse (heartbeat) but isn't breathing. For infants and children, you would give one breath every three seconds for the first minute then re-check the pulse. Continue rescue breathing at the same rate if you still had a pulse. If there's no pulse, go on to full CPR (breaths and compressions). Make sure you call 911 right away!

Do you ever perform chest compressions without rescue breathing?
No. Chest compressions are performed when administering CPR, which includes rescue breathing.

Is there much difference between performing CPR on an infant or a child?
The main difference is using your fingers to perform chest compressions on infants (under one year) and using the heel of your hand for children (over one year). This is simply because infants are much smaller. The rates are the same for both.

Should I stop doing CPR once I have started?
Try not to stop once you've started. Continue to perform CPR until medical help arrives, or until the infant or child recovers and starts breathing on his or her own.

Should I practice CPR?
Yes—but NEVER practice on live people. Practice CPR on approved training mannequins (special practice dolls) in a CPR class.

> **Remember!**
> **Don't delay in calling 911 for help. Continue CPR uninterrupted until emergency help arrives. Perform CPR only on a victim who is unconscious, not breathing and without a pulse.**

CPR—Cardiopulmonary Resuscitation

Be sure to give the parents a full report of your time with the children.

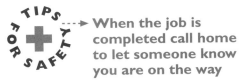

TIPS FOR SAFETY ---> When the job is completed call home to let someone know you are on the way

Time to Go Home

Your babysitting job is almost over. Now it's time to get ready for the parents to come home. About 15 minutes before you expect the parents to arrive, walk through the house and make sure everything is picked up. Clean up the kitchen. If the children are asleep, make sure they're tucked in. Fill out the "While You Were Away" form *(see page 102).*

When the parents arrive, give them your "While You Were Away" form—a full report of your time with the children. Parents really want to know what happened while they were away. Remember to note good times, any injuries (no matter

how small) and any disagreements.

Pass along any phone messages and report any visitors.

Figure out how long you worked. Calculate how much the parents owe you. If they pay you too little, tell them courteously that you think they made a mistake. Remind them how much your hourly rate is and how many hours you worked. If they pay you more than you expected, thank them for the tip.

Getting home safely

When the job is completed, call home to let someone know you're on your way. Never walk home alone in the dark. Be sure you have an escort to your front door.

Never get into the car with anyone who has been drinking or who acts suspiciously.
Call your parents for a ride or take a taxi. If anyone acts unusual or tries to touch you inappropriately, just look them straight in the eye and say, "Don't do that!" Get out of the car immediately. Tell your parents right away about any uncomfortable situations.

If you need help, but feel uncomfortable about giving your parents information in front of your clients, you may want to develop a code that only you and your parents know. For example, you could say "Hi, Mom. Is the key under the mat?" This could be a signal to your mother that really means, "Come and get me right away!" *Keep your code a secret.* Since you hopefully will never need to use the code, remind your parents before you leave so it will be fresh in everyone's minds—just in case.

As you leave

As you leave the babysitting job, tell the parents that you enjoyed spending time with their children and that you'd be happy to come again.

The more you know,
the more you'll grow
into the best babysitter
in your area.

TIPS FOR FUN! ···▶ **Play outdoor games**

A Final Note

You've now learned a lot about what it takes to be a babysitting pro. You have an idea of the different stages children go through and how to keep children healthy and safe. You know how to find babysitting jobs, you can determine which families will be good to work with and the key points of the babysitting job.

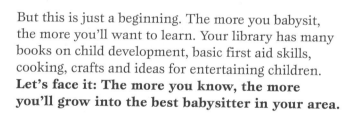

But this is just a beginning. The more you babysit, the more you'll want to learn. Your library has many books on child development, basic first aid skills, cooking, crafts and ideas for entertaining children. **Let's face it: The more you know, the more you'll grow into the best babysitter in your area.**

And who knows? The contacts you've made from babysitting might help you land other after-school or summer jobs as you grow older. You may find yourself starting a small business, planning parties for children, working as a camp counselor or as a volunteer with disabled or disadvantaged children. You might enjoy babysitting so much that you choose a lifelong career in teaching or childcare. The possibilities for people who genuinely love children are endless.

Be dedicated to becoming a real babysitting pro. You may be pleasantly surprised—both short-term and long-term—by the rewards!

Are you ready to start babysitting?

To find out, take this self-exam and test your knowledge. There are 20 multiple choice and 10 true or false questions. For some questions, more than one answer is correct, so be sure to select all answers that apply. The answers can be found in this section.

The purpose of this quiz is to help you understand your level of knowledge and areas where you may need additional training. It does not certify you or indicate qualifications. **It is important that you take a course in proper first aid and safety so you can have a clear understanding of the issues you will face in babysitting.**

Babysitter Quiz

Multiple choice quiz

1. **When changing a baby's diaper, all of the following are true *except*:**
   a. Assemble all supplies needed before changing a diaper.
   b. Find out from the parents the routine for diaper changes and how to dispose of soiled diapers.
   c. Wash the diaper area thoroughly with a diaper wipe or soft wash cloth.
   d. Leave the baby on a changing table while you gather supplies.
   e. Choose a flat, comfortable surface to change a diaper.

2. **You have recently tucked Ralphy, age 5, into bed and now hear him call out to you that he is afraid of the dark and can't sleep. What should you do first?**
   a. Remind him that big boys are not supposed to be afraid, to quiet down because you have homework to do.
   b. Let him get up and watch TV until his parents come home at midnight.
   c. Turn on a night light, read a soothing story and stay with him until he falls asleep.
   d. Tell him to quit stalling and threaten to call his parents.

3. **It is time to make lunch for Sara, a toddler, and Sam, age 5. Circle three answers below to make this a safe experience for all of you.**
   a. Lock the children in their room while you prepare a meal.
   b. Make sure the children are safe in a high chair or at the table while you prepare the meal.
   c. Assemble all supplies then wash your hands before you get started.
   d. When cooking or boiling water, turn pot handles toward you for easy handling.
   e. When cooking or boiling water, cook on back burners and turn pot handles away from you for safety.

4. **Four-month-old Lester is crying. What can you do to soothe him?**
   a. Pick the infant up gently and cuddle.
   b. Check the diaper and change if soiled.
   c. Gently pat the infant's back to burp and release trapped air in the tummy.
   e. Check baby's routine and see if it is time for a feeding.
   f. All of the above.

5. **It's time for Lester's bottle. All of the following are true about feeding infants *except*:**
   a. Always hold a baby while bottle-feeding, supporting the head, neck and back.
   b. It is okay to prop a baby's bottle against a pillow during a feeding so you can have more time for clean up.
   c. Ask the parents their routine for feedings and location of supplies.
   d. Burp a baby during and after a feeding to release trapped air the baby might have swallowed.

6. **Stevie, age 3, watches mom leave and wants to go outside even though it's raining. He soon begins to cry and falls to the floor screaming and kicking. What should you do?**
   a. Let him go outside because you want to make a good impression.
   b. Yell at him; tell him he is a bad boy.
   c. Make sure he is safe and try to distract him with a favorite game, activity or toy.
   d. Lock him in his room, while you watch TV.

7. **You're asked to cook dinner as a part of the job but you have no experience at preparing or cooking a meal. What should you do?**
   a. Get out a cookbook and give it your best shot.
   b. Tell the parents you have no experience cooking and let them know what items you can fix that might appeal to the children.
   c. Call your mom and ask her to come over and cook.
   d. Ask the parents to order take-out because cooking is not in your job description.

8. **While on the job, a woman comes unexpectedly to the door and asks to visit with the children. She says she is an old friend of the family. What should you do?**
   a. Ask the kids what they think.
   b. Let her in for just a short period of time.
   c. Politely ask the women to wait outside while you call the parents (or your parents) for permission.
   d. Let her in to use the phone and call the parents.

9. **You know that children and infants can drown in the smallest amounts of water. The best single protection against drowning is:**
   a. Teaching infants and children how to swim.
   b. Constant babysitter or adult supervision.
   c. Life jackets—Type PFD-3.

10. **Larry, age 5, has a nosebleed. Most nosebleeds can easily be stopped if you:**
    a. Lay the child down for a few minutes until he calms down.
    b. Give the child a Popsicle to suck on.
    c. Have the child blow his nose, then apply ice to the back of the neck.
    d. Apply gentle pressure to the nose for 5-10 minutes while the child sits up in a position of comfort.

11. **Ninth-month-old Emily is crying. She looks sick, feels hot to touch and refuses her next feeding. What should you do now?**
    a. Contact her parents, remove warm clothing and keep her comfortable.
    b. Call 911 for emergency medical support.
    c. Wait for symptoms to worsen before notifying the parents.

12. **Seven-year-old Sara was running barefoot outside and has just cut her foot. What is your first move?**
    a. Give medicine to decrease the pain.
    b. Use a clean cloth to apply pressure over the area to stop the bleeding.
    c. Elevate her foot.
    d. Apply pressure points to her ankle.

13. **A two-year-old reaches up to the hot stove and plays pat-a-cake with the burner. The young child's hand is red with blisters. What is your next step?**
   a. Offer plenty of water and juices.
   c. Get the burn under cool (not icy) water to decrease pain and swelling, and call for advice.
   c. Apply a large pat of butter to soothe the burn.
   d. Cover the burn with a cool-looking bandage.

14. **Susie has just fallen from the swing set and landed on her head. You run to her and find her on her side, confused, breathing fast, with a small bump on the side of her head. What can you do?**
   a. Elevate her legs and place a warm cloth across her forehead.
   b. Call 911 for emergency medical help and follow their instructions! Reassure the child and monitor her breathing until help arrives.
   c. There is nothing you can do.

15. **You are babysitting for the Smith family when you notice black smoke and flames coming from the basement. What should you do?**
   a. Attempt to put the fire out with a garden hose.
   b. Get the children and yourself out of the house and call 911 from a neighbor's house.
   c. Call your parents.
   d. Check the smoke detector.

16. **A toddler comes up to you with an empty bottle of pills and asks for more candy. You suspect a poisoning. What is your next move?**
   a. Wait for symptoms.
   b. Call 911 or poison control—NOW—for advice.
   c. Make the child vomit.

17. **The phone rings while you are giving three-year-old Lauren a bath. What should you do?**
   a. Take a break to answer the phone since it might be the parents.
   b. Ignore the phone call and stay with the child at all times during a bath.
   c. Tell the child to get out of the tub while you answer the phone.

18. **What phone number should you call in a serious emergency?**
   a. 90210
   b. Your parents phone number.
   c. 911—Fire, Police and Medical.
   d. Other_____ .

19. **Five-year-old Nick is having a snack and begins to cough forcefully. You should:**
   a. Stay nearby, be ready to help, but do not interfere with his coughing to clear his airway. When in doubt, call for advice.
   b. Immediately perform abdominal thrusts since he is choking and can't breathe.
   c. Slap his back firmly and continuously to help him stop.

20. **Now that you know a lot about babysitting, how should you get a job?**
   a. Advertise at the grocery store, laundry mats and in newspapers.
   b. Talk with people you know like neighbors, relatives and friends of the family. Get your parents to help you.
   c. Pass out flyers to everyone you meet.

Multiple choice answers

1. (d) Never leave a baby unattended on a changing table because an infant could fall off. Assemble all supplies needed before changing a diaper.

2. (c) A child who is afraid needs your attention. Tender, loving care will go a long way in calming a child's fears and increase their trust in you.

3. (b,c,e) When preparing a meal, make sure the children are safe, assemble all necessary supplies, and wash your hands.

4. (e) Don't panic if a baby cries—it's the baby's only way to communicate. Crying can mean all kinds of things such as loneliness, hunger, a dirty diaper, ready for a nap or time to be held. Check out crying with gentleness and when you don't know what to do call the parents.

5. (b) To avoid accidental choking, never prop a bottle on a pillow or towel while feeding the baby. Feeding is a social time for the baby and requires your undivided attention. Always hold a small infant in your arms during a bottle-feeding, with the baby's neck supported and head elevated.

6. (c) When children are separated from their parents they can experience frustration which can lead to a temper tantrum. Distraction to a favorite activity, toy or game can help. Be calm, supportive and make sure the child is safe.

7. (b) Don't be afraid to tell parents if you don't feel qualified to cook or take on unfamiliar tasks. The children's safety, as well as your own, are your top priority. Ask your parents to teach you how to do unfamiliar jobs or where you can get experience.

8. (c) Never let an unexpected visitor in the house when you are alone with the children, even if the person claims to be a relative. Think safety first. Call the parents or your parents for instructions.

9. (b) Constant babysitter or adult supervision is necessary around water. If you can't swim, don't have CPR training or have too many kids to watch, the safest thing to do is to tell the parents you don't feel qualified to take on this task.

10. (d) Stop the bleeding by using a clean cloth or tissue to apply direct pressure to the nose for 5-10 minutes. Discourage the child from blowing his or her nose after bleeding has stopped. If you can't stop the bleeding, make sure you get advice.

11. (a) When a baby is sick, especially if fever or other signs of illness, contact the parents or your parents for advice.

12. (b) Use a clean cloth to apply pressure over the area and stop the bleeding. Get advice if you can't stop the bleeding or the cut looks serious.

13. (b) Get the burn area under cool (not icy) water to decrease pain and swelling, and call for advice. Do not try to pop the blisters or apply medicines.

14. (b) When a child takes a bad fall, has trouble breathing, experiences unconsciousness, confusion, or has a serious injury to the body, it is important to seek emergency medical attention (911). Stay on the line and follow the medical team's instructions. The parents should be contacted as soon as possible. This is a situation you should not try to handle by yourself.

15. (b) Get the children and yourself out of the house and call 911 from a neighbor's. Because fire spreads quickly, don't try to put out the flames yourself, you may only have minutes to get everyone out safely.

16. (b) If you suspect that a child has inhaled or swallowed a poisonous substance such as a liquid, plant, gas or pill—don't wait for symptoms to occur. Get emergency help immediately! Call 911 for help or the poison center and follow their instructions.

17. (b) Nothing should distract you when you are caring for children around water. If the phone rings, don't answer it. They will call back.

18. (c) By calling 911 you can receive access to Fire, Police and Medical support. When in doubt, call for help, especially if you are unsure what to do or can't tell if a situation is serious.

19. (a) Coughing helps to clear our airway of unwanted objects. Be ready to help, but do not interfere with good coughing by slapping them too hard on the back or putting your fingers in their mouth. When in doubt, call for advice (911).

20. (b) Get advice from your parents on where to start looking for jobs and what kind of jobs you can take. Talk with friends of the family and relatives. It won't be long before the word gets out and you'll have lots of job opportunities.

Babysitting tips

✤ Never tell anyone you are alone with the children.

✤ Emergency numbers are important, especially a parent contact number.

✤ It is your job to follow the family routine set down by the parents. Ask the parent if you have any questions.

✤ Don't try to handle any emergency by yourself. Get help!

✤ Balloons and scissors are unsafe toys for infants and toddlers.

✤ Both the kids and parents will love you for giving your full attention to the kids, following the house rules and asking for help when you don't know what to do!

✤ Friends and telephones distract you from watching the children.

✤ The job goes smoother when you get a home tour.

✤ Everyone should know simple first aid skills. Take a class!

✤ Call your parents for a ride home if you don't feel safe. Talk with your parents so you'll know what to do.

Home survey and job instruction forms are very helpful. Make copies of the forms for future use.

Form

Write letters or make notecards

First Visit Home Survey

Make Copies! *Use a copy of this form on your first visit with a new family to help you get acquainted and learn any special situations or instructions before you begin working for them.*

Name of parent(s) _____

Address _____

Home phone _____ Work phone _____

City/State _____

Nearest cross street _____

Directions to home _____
_____

Names/ages of children: Allergies/special conditions

_____   _____

_____   _____

_____   _____

_____   _____

_____   _____

Date of visit _____ Parent location/phone _____ Sitter fee _____

Parent instructions

Have parent fill in the instructions.

Locate the following and get instructions when needed:

Alarms _____   Favorite toys, books or songs _____

Appliances _____   _____

Baby supplies _____   Fire extinguisher _____

Bedrooms _____   Flashlight _____

Diaper changes _____   Food _____

Doors, locks and telephones _____   House key _____

Clothing (extra) _____   Kitchen supplies _____

Exits _____   Pets _____

First aid kit _____   Play rooms _____

continued on back

First Visit Home Survey
continued

House rules

Bedtime rituals _____

Friends who may visit _____

How to handle arguments _____

Meal times & suggestions _____

Naps _____

Off limit areas _____

Outdoor rules _____

Snacks & drinks _____

Special comfort measures _____

How to handle temper tantrums _____

TV rules _____

Emergency information

Home address _____

Nearest cross street _____ Home phone _____

Police _____

Fire _____

Medic _____

House alarm instructions _____

Recent illnesses _____

Family doctor _____

Nearest hospital _____

Nearest safe neighbors _____

Nearest relative _____

Dentist _____

Veterinarian _____

Special situations/allergies _____

_____

Today's Job—
Information & Instructions

Use copies of this form to keep important information handy for each job. Have parent help fill it in.

Date _____ Time of job _____ Sitter fee per hour _____

Names & ages of children _____

_____

Name of parent(s) _____

Home phone _____ Work phone _____

Address _____ City/State _____

Nearest cross street _____

The parent(s) will be at _____ Phone _____

House rules

Today's instructions _____

_____

_____

Snack time _____ Bedtime _____

Meal time _____ Friends who may visit _____

Nap time _____ _____

Emergency information & phone numbers

Police _____ Fire _____ Medic _____

Family doctor _____ Phone _____

Nearest hospital _____ Phone _____

Nearest safe neighbors _____ Phone _____

Nearest relative _____ Phone _____

Dentist _____ Phone _____

Veterinarian _____ Phone _____

Allergies _____

Medical conditions _____

Recent illnesses _____

What Happened While You Were Away

Take a copy of this form to each babysitting job to help keep track of what happens during each sit and to keep the parents informed.

Babysitter _____ Date _____

For the parent: Thanks for choosing me to babysit. Here are messages and important details that occurred while you were away.

Phone calls

Full name _____ Phone _____
Message _____
_____

Full name _____ Phone _____
Message _____
_____

Full name _____ Phone _____
Message _____
_____

Full name _____ Phone _____
Message _____
_____

How the children and I spent our time

The children were fed at: _____

The children were in bed at: _____

The baby last ate at: _____

The last diaper change was at: _____

Boo-boos and accidents: _____

_____

_____

We spent our time doing: _____

_____

_____

Problems or questions that occurred: _____

_____

_____

Consent for Emergency Medical Treatment

It is important to have signed permission for medical treatment if an emergency situation occurs and the parents are not available. Below is a sample form parents can use to authorize treatment for their children in their absence. You can give the signed form to medical personnel when needed. Use a separate form for each child and update annually.

I/We, parent(s) or legal guardian(s) of _____ a minor, do
child's name

hereby authorize _____ as my/our agent(s) to arrange for
day care provider, babysitter, relative or other

routine or emergency medical/dental care and treatment necessary to preserve the health of my/our

child. I/We hereby voluntarily consent to care, including diagnostic procedures, surgical and medical

treatment, blood transfusions, x-ray examinations and anesthetic, by authorized members on the

medical staff of hospital or by _____ phone _____ (my family doctor)

as their professional judgment deems necessary.

Name of legal guardian(s) _____

Address _____

Day phone _____ Evening phone _____

Health insurance carrier _____ Group # _____

I/We have read this form and certify that I/we understand its contents.

Signature _____ Date _____

Signature _____ Date _____

Child's medical information

Age _____ Height _____

Weight _____ Date of birth _____

Child's allergies (medication & food):

_____

_____

Medicines child is taking: _____

_____

Immunizations current: _____
yes or no

Date of last tetanus booster: _____

Please describe any medical condition this child

currently has and how it is treated:

_____

_____

_____

_____

_____

_____

Notes

Add important details or your creative ideas here.

....

....

....

....

....

....

....

....

....

....

....

....

....

....

....

....

....

....